learning
together and alone

cooperation, competition, and individualization

DAVID W. JOHNSON / ROGER T. JOHNSON
University of Minnesota

PRENTICE-HALL, INC., Englewood Cliffs, New Jersey

Library of Congress Cataloging in Publication Data
JOHNSON, DAVID W.
        Learning together and alone.
        Bibliography: p.
        1. Lesson planning.   2. Classroom management.
I. Johnson, Roger T.   joint author.
II. Title.
LB1027.J54   371.1'02   74-28260
        ISBN 0-13-527952-6
        ISBN 0-13-527945-3 pbk.

This book is dedicated to our wives
Linda Mulholland Johnson
Annette Earle Johnson

10   9   8   7   6   5   4   3   2   1

Printed in the United States of America

Prentice-Hall International, Inc., *London*
Prentice-Hall of Australia, Pty. Ltd., *Sydney*
Prentice-Hall of Canada Ltd., *Toronto*
Prentice-Hall of India Private Limited, *New Delhi*
Prentice-Hall of Japan, Inc., *Tokyo*

contents

preface

As you may have surmised, we are brothers, and as such we are very
familiar with competition. For some years as we were growing up we
raced to see who would get through a door first, measured to see who got
more cake (or more of anything), and argued to see who would sit by the
window in the car. One incident we both remember vividly is the corncob
fight. For a few years while we were growing up in Indiana, we lived (and
worked!) on our grandfather's farm. We regularly practiced our accuracy
with corncobs, and more than occasionally we practiced on each other. In
one of these desperate battles, we had each gathered a large feed sack full
of corncobs and were flinging and dodging through the barn. When the
older one of us gained the upper hand, as he usually did, the younger
brother scampered up the ladder into the hayloft, taking a well-placed cob
in the seat of his pants. The hayloft advantage provided a problem for the
older brother as he was nipped a couple of times without even coming close
to his opponent. So taking a corncob between his teeth, he started up the
ladder (the only way to the loft). As he got about halfway up, he realized
he was getting pelted with more cobs than can be thrown at one time and
looked up to see the younger brother standing at the top of the ladder
shaking out his bag of corncobs and enjoying himself immensely. The
tables turned, however, when the older brother reached the top of the ladder and the younger brother discovered he was out of corncobs. Then it
was the younger brother's turn to be pelted as he crouched in the hay while
the older brother let him have it—one by one. We still argue about who
got the most out of the battle, the brother shooting the waterfall of corncobs down the ladder or the brother delivering the one-by-one pelting in
the hayloft.

v

We are sure that people who knew us then are genuinely surprised to see us cooperating on this book and in the related workshops for teachers that we conduct. It should not be a surprise. The ideas presented here on how to recognize inappropriate competition and facilitate productive cooperation are important enough even for two brothers to cooperate in presenting them. We are also accidentally, but admirably, suited to work together on this topic. David struggled through graduate school at Columbia University, gaining the skills of an academic social psychologist, and Roger, after teaching several years at the elementary school level, took the easy route through the University of California at Berkeley as a part-time staff member in teacher education. With the years of classroom teaching experience and the research and writing in social psychology represented by our combined backgrounds and brought together at the University of Minnesota, we readily recognized the potential of this conceptual scheme—structuring learning in ways consistent with instructional aims.

We aren't against competition (although the literature and research on competition are damaging to its reputation). We are against *inappropriate competition*; and most of the competition in classrooms is inappropriate. We are for cooperation, not only because the sharing, helping, communicating, and mutual concern aspects of it are consonant with our values but also because the research supports its use in a large number of situations. All the research we have reviewed, the research we have conducted, and our own instincts indicate that cooperation is the appropriate goal structure for most instructional situations. It also seems to be the least talked about, if not the least used, goal structure in schools. Individualization is, in some places, touted as a replacement for competition as the appropriate way to learn in schools. Students working on individually assigned tasks at their own pace, toward a set goal, instead of competing against each other, is attractive to teachers, but the overuse of the individualistic goal structure is hard on teachers, requires a mountain of materials, and is described by many students as the "lonely" curriculum. The basic social competencies needed to interact effectively with other persons, furthermore, are completely ignored under an individualistic goal structure. We believe that all three goal structures should be used, and that students need to learn how to function in all three. Students should master the skills to compete with enjoyment, to work individually on a task until it's completed, and to cooperate effectively with others to solve problems. Perhaps just as important, students should know *when* to compete, work on their own, or cooperate. The greatest need in classrooms is the carefully planned cooperative goal structure, which becomes the framework within which competition and individualization take place. We will cover a lot of pages on cooperation.

In our work with teachers in goal structuring workshops and in our own classes at the University of Minnesota, we have found a few obstacles that hinder implementation. First, teachers often do not realize the enormous potential that facilitating appropriate goal structures has for their classroom. The research is clear (see Appendix A). Achievement will go up, attitudes will become more positive, missing skills will be mastered when goal structures are used appropriately. After all, goal structures concentrate on what is the most powerful variable in the learning situation: the interaction patterns and interdependencies of the students as they work toward a goal. The second obstacle to recognizing immediately the importance of using cooperation as well as competitive and individualized activities is the extensive and powerful mythology that surrounds competition. How many times have you heard a version of Social Darwinism that suggests that "it's a dog-eat-dog world" or "a survival of the fittest society" or "students need to learn how to compete so they can survive in the business world." Even the business world does not believe that the world is savagely competitive. As a social psychologist with management training, David could spend much of his time teaching people in business and industry how to reduce inappropriate competition and increase cooperation in their companies. Society cannot be described as competitive; it is by definition cooperative, a point that will be examined in detail in Chapter 3. Within the cooperative framework of society, however, there is competition, sometimes too much.

Another obstacle we have observed is the "I'm already doing that" feeling that many teachers have when we describe cooperation. If you really are doing it as well as it can be done, much of this book will not be useful. Yet frequently we find that teachers who say (or think) they are using goal structures appropriately are surprised by certain aspects of each when these goal structures are carefully described from a social psychological point of view and when the steps for implementing and monitoring them are explained (see Chapters 4, 5, 7, and 8). Finally, the past educational history of many students and teachers is such that they find cooperating within the school rather strange and difficult. Our own students seem relieved when they find that they are not going to have to compete against each other, and a sigh of relief seems to go through the classroom when the cooperative approach is announced. Students are, however, usually somewhat reluctant at first to cooperate with each other and tend to work individualistically when they should be cooperating. It takes some relationship building and trust development before they are able to share ideas and help each other effectively to produce a true group effort. Your students may have some of the same attitudes (so may the teachers in your school) and, if they do, you may need to teach and encourage the skills needed to work together (see Chapter 6).

We wish we could be with you as you implement appropriate goal structures in your instructional program. We would like to help. For most of you, this book and the ideas shared here are the best we can do. We assume your classes will blossom as our own have and as those of teachers near us have. One thing is for sure, for those of you who want to match appropriate student interaction patterns with instructional goals and want to move to a predominantly cooperative classroom, the rationale for doing so is here, and you will be able to discuss goal structuring fluently with any-one. We hope that enough of the strategies are here also, but implementing ideas is your profession and if something is left out, we trust you to find and include it. Above all, enjoy the process. Practice your own skills as you encourage them in your students. You may even try a little cooperating with fellow teachers! In fact, we suggest that the best way to work with the ideas in this book is to approach the task cooperatively with a friend and fellow teacher to share thoughts and successes with. Enjoy yourself, per-severe, and accept any resulting success with some modesty.

Thanks are due to many people for their help in writing this book and preparing the manuscript. We owe much to many social psychologists who have conducted research and formulated theory in this area. We owe much to the teachers who have listened to our "bridge building" and given us help in "reconstructing" when we needed it. We owe much to our stu-dents who have been patient with our enthusiasm and helpful in chal-lenging and implementing our ideas. Finally, we owe much to our wives for making our lives truly cooperative.

ROGER T. JOHNSON
DAVID W. JOHNSON

key to basic information on each goal structure

	Cooperation	Competition	Individualization
	pages	*pages*	*pages*
Definition	7	7	7
Research	25–37 185–199	25–37 185–199	25–37 185–199
Myths	54–56	39–49	49–54
Selection *	62, 65–66	60–63, 66	62–64, 66
Implementation	77–79 82–83, 84 90–93	77, 78 81, 83, 84 86–90	77, 78, 80 83, 84
Skills	99–111	111–112	112–113
Monitoring	123–124 128–142 145–148	125–126 128–141 145–148	124–125 128–141 145–148
Evaluating	158–170	158–170	158–170

* Chapter 7 summarizes the teacher's role, including selection and implementation.

effective
learning
$=$

working
together
to solve
problems

$+$
competing
with
enjoyment

$+$
working on
your own
to complete
a task

ONE
increasing teachers' effectiveness and fun

INSTRUCTION

Mastering this book will make teaching easier, more productive, and more enjoyable. By systematically using cooperative, competitive, and individualized goal structures, a teacher can improve his * relationships with students and influence the processes of learning and the affective and cognitive outcomes of instruction. Goal structures are the most important instructional variable in the classroom; a teacher can have more impact upon learning and classroom life through using goal structures appropriately than through engaging in any other set of behaviors. But before we can discuss the use of goal structures to facilitate instruction, we must define the basic processes of a school and of a teacher's professional life: education, learning, and instruction.

* Throughout this book, the pronouns *he, she, his, hers,* are used randomly.

1

◇◇◇

The purpose of schools is to:

a. keep children off the street in order to protect society.

b. keep children out of the home in order to protect the parents.

c. keep teachers off the street in order to protect society.

d. keep teachers out of their homes in order to protect their children.

e. keep school administrators rich by paying them large salaries.

f. keep teachers poor by paying them small salaries.

g. develop each student to maximum capacity as a productive and happy member of society.

h. drive teachers crazy by giving them too many students, too few materials, and impossible tasks and by yelling for accountability.

i. All of the above.

j. None of the above.

k. Some of the above.

◇◇◇

Why do we have schools? What is supposed to happen to students within a school? What are the teacher's responsibilities within a school? Certainly there is general agreement that schools are created to socialize students into the attitudes, capabilities, and skills they need to be productive and self-actualizing members of society. Schools are created to educate students, and students are supposed to become educated as they move through the instructional program of a school. A large part of a teacher's role is to ensure that students are in fact educated by the school's instructional program. But what is education, what is learning, and what is instruction?

Education is the structuring of a situation in ways that help students change, through learning, in intentional (and sometimes unintentional) ways. *Learning* is a change within the student that is brought about by the instructional program of a school. Changes that do *not* count as learning are: changes in performance due to reflexes such as the knee jerk, eye blink, breathing, or nausea; maturation or growth changes such as sexual or conceptual development that is relatively independent of specific learning conditions; and temporary states of the student due to fatigue, habituation, drugs, or fright. Only changes that are due to experience are called learning. As far as teaching is concerned, *learning* is a change observed in the student after instruction has taken place. Teachers assess learning by observing the student's performance within a structured situation; the student's performance is observed, instruction is given, and the student's performance is observed again. If changes have taken place, the teacher concludes that learning has occurred. It should be remembered, however, that learning is a private process and can only be assessed by observing the student's performance. Performance and learning are not equivalent. A student can learn something and yet have a variety of other factors (such as a sudden onslaught of spring fever, school psychosis,* or the flu) interfere with his performance (causing him to receive a low score on a test). It should also be remembered that learning is usually a combination of (1) information or ideas, (2) feelings or emotions, and (3) muscular coordination or physical skills. Testing for knowledge will not indicate whether the student has learned to *like* to use the knowledge or is able to translate the knowledge into *behaviors* and applications. Finally, it is helpful to remember that although a teacher is able to facilitate the occurrence of learning, only the student can *cause* himself to learn. This point is summarized in the old saying of horses, "You can pitch your rider into the lake, but you can't make him swim." † In other words, worry about facilitating learning, not about causing or making students learn.

Teachers are expected to implement (and sometimes build) instructional systems so that student learning is facilitated. *Instruction* can be defined as the process of arranging the learning situation in such a way that student learning is facilitated. Theories of instruction prescribe procedures concerning the most effective way of facilitating student acquisition of knowledge, attitudes, and skills. Our theory of instruction states that successful instruction depends upon the following components:

1. Specifying desired outcomes for the students and setting appropriate instructional goals.
2. Implementing the appropriate goal structure; goal structures can be cooperative, competitive, or individualistic.
3. Assembling the instructional materials and resources needed to facilitate the desired learning.
4. Creating an instructional climate that facilitates the type of interaction among students and between students and teacher needed to achieve the instructional goals.

* School psychosis occurs when a student inexplicably becomes sick to his stomach during a lecture, begins to scream uncontrollably when entering the classroom, or goes into a catatonic trance while staring out the window.

† The authors once had a horse who spent several years trying to teach them how to swim by this method.

5. Assessing and providing feedback on students' progress toward the desired outcomes while instruction is underway.

6. Assessing and providing feedback on the intended and unintended outcomes of instruction; besides the sought-for outcomes, many times there are unanticipated outcomes; a teacher should be concerned with the actual consequences of an instructional program, irrespective of whether they are planned or expected.

HOW DO YOU TELL IF YOU ARE AN EFFECTIVE TEACHER?

Teaching effectiveness is the successful implementation of the components of instruction. Each component of instruction has its corresponding teacher skills. Teachers need to be skilled in setting instructional goals (see Johnson and Johnson, 1975, and Johnson, 1972, for a discussion of the skills in setting goals), implementing the appropriate goal structures, assembling the materials and resources students need to complete the instructional tasks, creating a facilitative learning climate, assessing and providing feedback on the students' progress while instruction is underway, and assessing and providing feedback on the intended and unintended consequences of instruction. *Of all the components of instruction, it is a teacher's skills in implementing the appropriate goal structures that are most important and which have been most ignored in teacher training programs.* For, as will be explained in this book, once the goal structures are correctly and appropriately implemented, many of the other components of instruction are more easy to manage. Conversely, if the goal structures are used inappropriately or are implemented incorrectly, the other components of instruction become increasingly difficult to manage. You can tell how effective a teacher you are by assessing your ability and skills in implementing each aspect of instruction.

◇◇◇

I have very high skills in:

_____setting instructional goals that are measurable and realistic (I usually know what I want to do and why, and I communicate it effectively to my students).

_____implementing the goal structures appropriately and correctly (I know when to use each goal structure, and I can set it up so that it works).

_____assembling needed resources and materials (I am ready for almost any request made by students, and I have a variety of resources to use).

_____creating a facilitative learning climate (I can promote comfortable relationships within the classroom and facilitate the communication and trust that increase learning).

_____assessing and providing feedback on student progress (I have mastered several procedures for accurately gaining information about the learning processes of students and can feed that information back to students in a constructive fashion).

_____assessing and providing feedback on student outcomes (I know what outcomes are consistent with the goals, and I have effective ongoing ways of accurately measuring these outcomes along with unanticipated outcomes).

◇◇

WHAT ARE GOAL STRUCTURES?

In a science class, students are working in small groups with a variety of experimental equipment, struggling to solve a puzzling problem concerning the differences among several white powders. The quality of the group report documenting their procedures and conclusions will determine how the students will be evaluated in the instructional unit. In another classroom, students are seated individually at their desks, working quietly on a programmed instructional unit dealing with the correct use of microscopes. Each person works by himself or herself and will be evaluated on the basis of how well the material is mastered. In a third classroom, students are working on their own, attempting to be the first to complete correctly a project on insects. They will be evaluated on how fast, in relation to the other students, they correctly complete the project. The faster students will be called "winners," and the slower students will be thought of as "losers."

In each of these classrooms the instructional activities are being conducted under a different goal structure. What is a goal structure? To answer that question, it is first necessary to define a goal. A _goal_ is a desired state of future affairs.* A learning goal may be the ability to spell a list of words, the successful completion of a mathematics problem, the solution of a puzzling problem through the application of inquiry methods, the completion of a scholarly theme of high quality, or the understanding of a set of basic concepts within a subject area. In discussing a goal, three things

* The younger of the two authors once had a goal to be taller than the older of the two authors (this was a competitive goal). Consequently, he missed reaching his full potential of 6 feet, 2 inches as he was pounded daily on the top of the head for several years until his growth was stunted.

need to be highlighted: first, the actual goal; second, the tasks the person must engage in to accomplish the goal; and third, the processes through which the person must relate to other learners in working toward task completion and goal accomplishment. Thus the goal may be mastering inductive methods of solving chemistry problems, the tasks may be a series of experiments utilizing certain logical principles and laboratory apparatus, and the processes of interaction with other students may be the sharing of information, materials, ideas, and helpful hints concerning the best procedures to use.

Learning is based primarily upon a person's commitment to accomplish her or his learning goals. It is a person's goals that direct and moti-

◇◇◇

Our horse, Maud, could give a fantastic ride! She did not like leaving the barn, and we would have to fight her all the time to get her any distance away from it. In her attempts to return to the barn, Maud would try to scrape us off on fences as we rode away from the barn. Once we did turn back toward the barn, however, we got the ride of our lives (the younger author never seemed to remember to duck as Maud flew through the barn door)! The point is that Maud was not committed to leaving the barn, but she had a strong commitment to return to it. All teachers have seen the difference between students who are committed to learning goals and those who are not. If students are not committed to instructional goals, they are like Maud going away from the barn. If students are committed to instructional goals, they are like Maud returning to the barn. Take the advice of the younger author and duck for the barn door when you successfully "turn on" your students.

◇◇◇

vate her behavior. As the person commits herself to achieving a certain goal, an inner tension is aroused and continues until the goal has been accomplished or until some sort of psychological closure is achieved concerning the goal. It is this inner tension that motivates the person to work toward goal accomplishment. Thus when a student commits herself to mastering the inductive procedures necessary to solve chemistry problems, she sets up an internal tension system that makes her restless and dissatisfied until she has successfully mastered the procedures or until she decides that she no longer wishes to learn the procedures. A person's commitment to accomplish learning goals depends upon several factors, such as (1) how attractive or desirable the goal seems, (2) how likely it seems that it can be accomplished, (3) how challenging the goal is (a moderate risk of failure is more challenging than a high or low risk of failure), (4) whether or not the person is able to tell when the goal has been achieved, (5) the satisfaction or reward the person expects to feel when the goal is achieved, and (6) the ways in which the person will relate to other people in working toward the accomplishment of the goals.

Given that a goal is a desired state of future affairs and that the person's commitment to her learning goals motivates her learning, what is a goal structure? When different students are all working on learning goals relating to the same instructional activities, they are related by the overall goal structure set up by the teacher. A *goal structure* specifies the type of interdependence existing among students. It specifies the ways in which students will relate to each other and to the teacher in working toward the accomplishment of instructional goals. There are three types of goal structures: cooperative, competitive, and individualistic. When students are working together to find what factors make a difference in how long a candle burns in a quart jar, they are in a cooperative goal structure. A *cooperative goal structure* exists when students perceive that they can obtain their goal if, and only if, the other students with whom they are linked can obtain their goal (Deutsch, 1949a). Since the goal of all the students is to make a list of factors that influence the time the candle burns, the goal of all the students has been reached when they generate a list. A cooperative goal structure requires the coordination of behavior necessary to achieve the mutual goal. If one student achieves the goal, all students with whom the student is linked achieve the goal. When students are working to see who can build the best list of factors influencing the length of time a candle will burn in a quart jar, they are in a competitive goal structure. A *competitive goal structure* exists when students perceive that they can obtain their goal if, and only if, the other students with whom they are linked fail to obtain their goal (Deutsch, 1949a). If one student turns in a better list than anyone else, all the other students have failed to achieve their goal. Competitive interaction is the striving to achieve one's goal in a way that blocks all others from achieving the goal. Finally, if students are all working independently to master an operation in mathematics, they are in an individualistic goal structure. An *individualistic goal structure* exists when the achievement of the goal by one student is unrelated to the achievement of the goal by other students; whether or not a student achieves her goal has no bearing upon whether other students achieve their goals. If one student masters the mathematics principle, it has no bearing upon whether other students successfully master the mathematics principle. Usually there is no student interaction in an individualistic situation, since each student seeks the outcome that is best for himself regardless of whether or not other students achieve their goals.

◇◇◇

When students commit themselves psychologically to achievement in school, important factors are how likely they are to be successful in achieving academic goals and how challenging academic goals are to them. When teachers "grade on a curve" and receiving an "A" is defined as being successful—i.e., the goal—the vast majority of students will not expect to achieve the goal whereas the high ability students may see the goal as being too easy to be challenging. Thus a teacher may lose most students because of a low likelihood of success and the superior students, whose resources make achievement too easy, all in one swoop!

Commitment to academic goals also requires that students perceive the goals as being desirable and that they feel some satisfaction when the goals are achieved. There is consistent evidence that when classrooms are structured competitively or individualistically, success at academic tasks has little value for many students (Coleman, 1959; Bronfenbrenner, 1970; Spilerman, 1971; DeVries et al., 1971). Receiving recognition from one's peers is a source of satisfaction, yet there is recent evidence (as well as ancient folklore) that success on academic tasks in a competitively structured classroom has a negative effect on a student's sociometric status in the classroom (Slavin, 1974). Doing well on frequently given quizzes resulted in losing friends!

The teacher's primary hope of inducing student commitment to academic goals is in structuring cooperative learning situations in the classroom. If you do not now believe it, keep reading, and by the time you finish this book you will!

◇◇◇

Consider the situation in which the teacher makes no attempt to implement any goal structure or in which he allows students to choose their own goal structure. When students are familiar with all three goal structures, have the skills to implement all three, and have experience working within each type of goal structure, they will probably be very good judges as to which goal structure is most desirable for accomplishing specified instructional goals. When students do not have past experience in each type of goal structure or do not have skills to implement successfully the three goal structures, an informed and free choice cannot take place. A person's conception of the alternatives in a situation depends upon his past experience and his perceptions of the situational constraints. If students have rarely experienced a goal structure other than interpersonal competition in school, they will tend to form competitive goal structures when left to their own devices. If all the other organizational pressures within the school are based upon the traditional interpersonal competitive goal structure, students will tend to behave competitively whenever they are left "free" to choose. Under such conditions no goal structure at all or a superficial choice among the three goal structures is to ask students subtly (or not so subtly) to place the traditional interpersonal competitive goal structure upon themselves.

<><><><><><><><><><><><><><><><><><><><><><><><><><><><><><><><><><><><>

Would each of these situations be cooperative, competitive, or individualistic?

1. Students writing themes on "What I Did Last Summer," which will be graded on a curve.
2. A group of students attempting to mark out and measure the difference between an acre and a hectare.
3. Students working independently to master a list of spelling words.
4. A student working with a slide rule to see if she can use it more proficiently than anyone else in the class.
5. Three students working together to survey their neighborhood to see if people are using less electricity than they did a year ago.
6. A student working through a programmed text on speaking Spanish.
7. Elementary school teachers decorating their rooms at the beginning of the school year.
8. Two brothers writing a book together.
9. A younger sister attempting to write a better book than her two older brothers.

<><><><><><><><><><><><><><><><><><><><><><><><><><><><><><><><><><><><>

WHAT IS THE NEED FOR THIS BOOK?

Of all the components of instruction, goal structures are the most important. Yet the whole idea of goal structures has never been clearly explained to teachers, and most teachers have not received any training in the skills of implementing and using goal structures. The current use of goal structures for instructional purposes is usually inappropriate, and even when goal structures are appropriately used they are often implemented poorly and ineffectively. This book will give a detailed explanation as to when each type of goal structure should be used and how each may be properly set up and monitored.

The traditional goal structure used in the vast majority of schools in the United States is the interpersonal goal structure in which students are expected to outperform their peers. There is considerable evidence (see Appendix A) that: (1) most students perceive school as being competitive, (2) American children are more competitive than are children from other countries, (3) American children become more competitive the longer they are in school or the older they become, (4) Anglo-American children are more competitive than American children, with other ethnic backgrounds, for instance, Mexican-American or black-American children, and (5) urban children are more competitive than rural children. The tendency for American children to compete often interferes with their capacity for adaptive, cooperative problem solving. The socialization of American children into competitive attitudes and orientations is so pervasive that Staub (1971) found that American children often believe that helping a person in distress is inappropriate and is disapproved of by others! American children seldom cooperate spontaneously (in comparison with children from other cultures), apparently because the environment provided for these children is barren of experiences that would sensitize them to the possibility of cooperation. Nelson and Kagan (1972) state that most American children engage in irrational and self-defeating competition and the Anglo-American child (in comparison with children from other cultures) is even willing to reduce his own reward in order to reduce the reward of a peer:

> Anglo-American children are not only irrationally competitive, they are almost sadistically rivalrous. Given a choice, Anglo-American children took toys away from their peers on 78% of the trials even when they could not keep the toys for themselves. Observing the success of their actions, some of the children gloated, "Ha! Ha! Now you won't get a toy." Rural Mexican children in the same situation were rivalrous only half as often as the Anglo-American child.

Thus there is overwhelming evidence that American children are highly competitive, that they do not receive the type of experiences that would sensitize them to the possibility of cooperation, and that schools promote this irrational competition. Yet there is solid evidence (see Appendix A) that when the different structures are explained students actually prefer cooperative goal structures for school work! Students are *not* learning within the goal structure they prefer, and they are being greatly affected by the pervasiveness of interpersonal competition in our society. Most teachers, furthermore, do not structure specific competitive conditions except during examinations; at other times a diffuse and ambiguous competitive climate is maintained by emphasizing that students should work independently while trying to do better than their peers. This ambiguous competitive climate has several destructive consequences (see Chapter 3).

◇◇

"Competing with and defeating an opponent is one of the most widely recognized aspects of interpersonal interaction in our society. The language of business, politics, and even education is filled with "win-lose" terms. One "wins" a promotion or a raise, "beats" the opposition, "outsmarts" a teacher, puts competitors "in their place." In an environment that stresses winning, it is no wonder that competitive behavior persists where it is not appropriate."

D. W. Johnson and F. P. Johnson, 1975

◇◇

This book is needed to present clearly the theory underlying the use of goal structures by teachers and the procedures and skills for doing so, and to correct the present situation in which most teachers use interpersonal competition inappropriately and poorly and do not encourage the appropriate use of all three goal structures. There is widespread dissatisfaction with the use of competition to motivate learning, and individualized programs are being presented as an alternative, yet research indicates that individualistic goal structures are useful only under a limited set of conditions. We will review those conditions in Chapter 4. The most under-utilized goal structure (and the most valuable) is cooperation. Although cooperation is a prerequisite for effective problem solving and for the learning of complex material, and although noted authorities such as Coleman (1972) state that a major goal of the school must be to educate students to work cooperatively with others, the procedures for implementing cooperation have never been clearly spelled out. In this book we shall specify the conditions under which cooperative goal structures should be used and explain the specific procedures for implementing them in the classroom. After mastering this material you will never again wonder how to reduce competitive dynamics among students * or how to increase students' cooperative interaction with each other and with you, the teacher; you will know how!

Why has cooperation been ignored in teacher training and learning? Why didn't someone write this book twenty years ago? The answer is found

---

* For a heart-rending but true life story of the misery of having to live with rabid competition among children, the reader may write to our parents, Mr. & Mrs. Roger W. Johnson, 1217 Wildwood Lane, Muncie, Indiana.

Do we need to educate students to be winners? Is this a dog-eat-dog competitive world in which only the fittest survive and therefore students need to be tough competitors?

_____Yes   _____No

Do we need to educate students to be rugged individualists? Does everyone need to be able to survive on his own, to live without bending to the roar of the crowd?

_____Yes   _____No

◇◇

Do we need to educate students to work with others under the discipline imposed by a common task and purpose? Is striving toward common goals the most important and pervasive activity of educated persons? Is it true that civilization exists only while humans strive to achieve common goals? Is it true that without high levels of cooperation our species is doomed?

_____Yes   _____No

◇◇

in the fact that over 90 percent of all human interaction is cooperative! We will discuss this fact in more detail in Chapters 2 and 3, but let it suffice to say that cooperation to a human is like water to a fish; it is so pervasive that it remains unnoticed. Cooperation is a *nonconscious* goal of interaction; after all, how could any interaction take place without enough cooperation to establish communication, set norms for behavior, and agree upon goals. The urge to cooperate is so pervasive that it is usually nonconscious in the sense that no alternative seems possible. All competition and individualistic behavior take place within a broader cooperative framework. *Cooperation is the forest, competition and individualism are but trees.*

There are other reasons why this book is needed. Several current educational trends highlight the necessity of using goal structures appropriately in order to accomplish instructional goals. In the following sections we shall discuss in detail each of these trends; they are

1. The concern that instructional methods be based upon the theory and research of the social sciences rather than upon fads and salesmanship of advocates (education has a long history of adopting instructional procedures on the basis of what is in fashion rather than on the basis of what actually works).
2. The movement toward a more humanizing educational experience for students and teachers.
3. The emphasis on teaching the skills needed for problem solving rather than on teaching information and facts.
4. The interest in open classrooms and open education.

RESEARCH AVAILABLE FROM THE SOCIAL SCIENCES

There is nothing more valuable than a theory that has been confirmed by research and can be implemented in a practical way. Education rests upon the assumption that the application of knowledge leads to productive problem solving and effective living. Yet in the past, educators did not fully utilize the knowledge of the social sciences in planning instructional methods and procedures. The considerable amount of research done on the use of cooperative, competitive, and individualistic goal structures in social psychology is summarized in Appendix A of this book. From that research the authors have built a practical theory that can be used by any teacher. *This book is one of the few to recommend educational practices based solidly upon research and verified theory.* It is one of a series of books aimed at applying social psychological knowledge to educational practice (see Johnson, 1972; Johnson and Johnson, 1975). The future of instruction and teaching rests upon the successful application of social science knowledge to instructional methods and procedures, and this book is an example of how such utilization is accomplished.

HUMANISTIC EDUCATION

The movement toward humanistic education is a major trend of education. In order to discuss this trend and indicate how the appropriate use of the three goal structures will relate to it, it is first necessary to define some concepts. *Humanism* is the use of reason in human affairs, applied in the service of compassion (Johnson, 1973a). *Humanistic education*, therefore, is education that promotes the compassionate use of reason in dealing with other humans, other living creatures, and inanimate nature. Since the compassionate use of reason in dealing with other humans is vital in the type of relationships created between students, teachers, principals, and other school personnel, *education needs to focus upon the attitudes, values, and beliefs that promote humane interaction and the skills and capacities needed for building and maintaining humanizing relationships.*

What is a humanizing relationship? How do you know one when you see it? A *humanizing relationship* is a relationship that reflects the qualities of kindness, mercy, consideration, tenderness, love, concern, compassion, cooperation, responsiveness, and friendship. In a humanizing relationship individuals are sympathetic and responsive to human needs, invest each other with the character of humanity, and treat and regard each other as human. It is the positive involvement with other people that we label humane. In a *dehumanizing relationship* persons are divested of those qualities that are uniquely human; they are turned into machines—treated in impersonal ways that reflect unconcern with human values. To be inhumane is to be unmoved by the suffering of others, to be cruel, brutal, and unkind.

Two major forces lead to dehumanization in the classroom. The first is the bureaucratic organizational structure of both the individual school and the school system. The second is the interpersonal competition goal structure within which most schooling takes place. Bureaucratic organizational structure promotes dehumanization by depersonalizing relationships, and competition (when overused and used inappropriately) promotes negative and destructive relationships among students. The destructive consequences of competition will be discussed at length in Chapter 3; only the dehumanizing effects of the bureaucratic organizational structure are discussed here.

Schools are typically highly bureaucratic organizations (Johnson, 1970). The bureaucratic organizational structure was invented to dehumanize relationships within organizations (Johnson, 1973a)! The bureaucratic organizations compare with previous methods of organizing work and effort exactly as does the machine with nonmechanical modes of production; the more perfect the bureaucracy, the more the bureaucracy is "dehumanized" and the more completely it succeeds in eliminating from official business love, hatred, and all purely personal, irrational, and emotional elements. A bureaucratic organization tends to view human beings as instruments designed to achieve ends considered by the organization to be more important than those of the individual. Bureaucracy promotes impersonality of relationships, segmentation of individuals, machine-like behavior with only a small part of a person involved in doing his job. Work competence is the major criterion for rewards.

How does this description of bureaucracies fit your experience as a student and as a teacher? Do the role definitions of "student" and "teacher" promote an impersonality that keeps emotional considerations from influencing role behavior (such as in the case of grading)? Is your behavior as a student or teacher organized by the role definition so that only a small part of you, as a person, is involved? Are you a replaceable part to be manipulated by others, or are you valued as someone who can never be replaced or duplicated? Are you rewarded only on the basis of competence? In your school, are there real friendships between students and teachers, or are friendships carefully contained to paternalistic caring on the part of the teacher, with a constant awareness by the student of who has the power and authority? Considering the qualities of humanizing relationships, do you have such relationships with others in your school and if so, with whom? Considering the qualities of dehumanizing relationships, do you have such relationships with others in your school and if so, with whom?

If education is to be humanized, much more attention needs to be paid to helping students develop the interpersonal skills needed to cooperate with one another and to build and maintain positive interpersonal relationships within the classroom. Through the appropriate use of the three goal structures and through an emphasis on cooperative interaction among students and between the students and the teacher, teachers can promote humanizing relationships within the classroom. In addition, a teacher should emphasize humanistic values (such as the appreciation and utilization of differences among individuals) and include them within the curriculum content aimed specifically at developing interpersonal skills. The attitudes, values, skills, and capacities for creating humanizing relationships will be discussed throughout this book.

So wherever I am, there's always Pooh, there's always Pooh and me. "What would I do," I said to Pooh, "If it wasn't for you?" and Pooh said, "True! It isn't much fun for one, but two can stick together," says Pooh, says he. "That's how it is," says Pooh.

A.A. Milne

PROBLEM SOLVING

An increasing emphasis in the schools is on encouraging students to function as problem solvers. The increasing amount of information on every subject and the rapid change in theory and orientations toward most subjects has made the learning of factual information obsolete. What a student learns as true in elementary school may be long-discarded myth by the time he enters graduate school. Thus, what is increasingly seen as important is the learning of problem-solving procedures and skills. Two basic points need to be made about problem solving. The first is that problem solving is not solely a cognitive activity. In successful problem solving, feelings, intuition, and hunches play an important part. In learning how to be a problem solver, a student needs to learn to recognize her feelings, tune in on her intuition, and follow up her hunches in ways that either confirm or disconfirm their validity. The affective side of learning, therefore, is an important aspect of problem solving. The second basic point is that problem solving is not a solitary activity. Almost all problem solving in our society takes place in groups, such as occupational work teams, families, and friendship groups. Problem solving is an inherently cooperative process in which several individuals join together to accomplish shared goals. Thus, in order for problem solving to take place, students must learn the interpersonal and group skills necessary. For skill-training programs, see Johnson (1972) and Johnson and Johnson (1975).

To become a problem solver, a student must develop skills in a process or procedure of problem solving. The most effective procedure for teaching problem solving is the inquiry or discovery method. There is a strong relationship between inquiry learning and cooperative learning structures. Although the literature on inquiry includes little direct reference to cooperation, methods books and transcripts of teacher activities emphasize cooperative processes in inquiry learning. They recommend that students work in small groups to solve problems—talking together and sharing information, generating alternative ideas, replicating each others' experi-

17

Once there was a little hand that could do many things.

 It could say "Stop!"

 It could say "OK."

 It could point to anything it wanted to (even though that's not always polite).

 It could scratch.

 It could say "Peace."

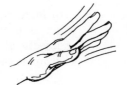 And it could wave goodbye.

 It could be strong, or very gentle.

 It could be scary, or stand at attention.

 But it couldn't make a sound.

 The hand became dejected and sad.

Then something happened—another hand appeared, and there was a wonderful noise. And that just goes to show you that it takes two hands to clap.

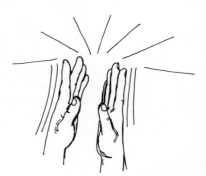

Adapted from skit on "Sesame Street."

ments and sharing data, inventing tests to try ideas, and sharpening up inferences about results. Then, in class discussions, there can be sharing between groups. Inquiring does not necessarily depend on a cooperative structure and can probably exist under a range of structures, but research indicates that achievement in terms of problem solving is facilitated by such cooperation (Watson and Johnson, 1972; Johnson and Johnson, 1974a). This material that describes cooperation as a classroom structure and the strategies for setting up a cooperative structure in the classroom will fill a gap in the current writing on inquiry teaching.

OPEN EDUCATION

One of the most exciting trends in education is toward open education, several themes of which relate specifically to the issue of goal structures:

Almost every critic of current school practices challenges the use of competition in schools; these criticisms have been discussed in a previous section of this chapter and will be further discussed in Chapter 3.

Advocates of open education recommend the changing of the physical arrangement of the classroom so that cooperative interaction among students is not only possible but more likely to happen.

The humanization of relationships among students is emphasized.

Problem-solving activities are emphasized.

Importance is put on affective outcomes of learning by which students develop positive attitudes and thereby become "life-long learners."

For a more elaborate discussion of open education see Johnson and Johnson (1974b).

The relationship between the cooperative goal structure and open education is apparent in the literature on open schools. Books and articles on the British infant school, where the open education movement originated, describe the use of multi-age groupings in which students are expected to learn from each other. Descriptions of open classrooms point out that cooperatively structured discussions are the rule. They emphasize the need for trust and openness and show how the interpersonal skills of teachers and students work to create an accepting learning environment. Perhaps the most important point in the literature on open education is the general agreement that the traditional competitive goal structure should be thrown out. There is no clear statement, however, on what goal structure should take its place. This book will present detailed instructions on how to implement cooperative goal structures as the major alternative to traditional interpersonal competition.

In visiting some British primary school classrooms and chatting with British teachers, it is evident that the move from formal to informal classrooms is partly a move away from competition as a dominant goal structure. These teachers talk a great deal about individualization as they pursue their skills programs and the topic work, or thematic curriculum, and move toward an integrated day. However, in watching the instructional situation, incidents of sharing and helping are numerous and students' efforts often result in a common project or paper. Without the carefully worked out, structured individualized currriculums available in this country, these classrooms seem to be moving more toward a cooperative goal structure than individualistic, and this is one of the most impressive aspects of these British classrooms for the visitor.

AUTHORS' BIAS

Before you continue reading this book, the authors wish to make their bias clear. We believe that cooperative, competitive, and individualistic goal structures are all appropriate and effective under different conditions, that educators should use all three goal structures depending upon their specific instructional objectives, and that students should be taught the basic skills necessary to function in all three types of situations. Much of the current literature on educational reform, however, is highly critical of competition, and where we sum up statements of others on the outcomes of competition, the critics' negative attitudes are inevitably reflected. This reflects the inappropriate use of competition rather than any inherently negative effects of competing. Since cooperation is both the most under-utilized goal structure used in current education practice, and probably the most important, it is highlighted in this book. In terms of instructional situations in most classrooms cooperation should be the most frequently used goal structure, individualistic goal structures used less often, and competition used least often. As you gain skill in using the three goal structures, you will soon come to realize why they are the most powerful influence on education within the classroom, and why mastering this book will make teaching easier, more productive, and more enjoyable.

Certainly, aggressiveness exists in nature, but there is also a healthy nonruthless competition, and there exist very strong drives toward social and cooperative behavior. These forces do not operate independently but together, as a whole, and the evidence strongly indicates that, in the social and biological development of all living creatures, of all these drives, the drive to cooperation is the most dominant, and biologically the most important. . . . It is probable that man owes more to the operation of this principle than to any other in his own biological and socal evolution.

Ashley Montagu, 1966

cooperation is basic to all human interaction
and provides the context
for competition and individualization

cooperation is the forest;
competition and individualization are but trees

TWO

goal structures, learning processes, and instructional outcomes

INTRODUCTION

Schooling is a social process in the sense that students are placed in groups called "classes" and a teacher is given the responsibility of managing the instruction for a number of students at the same time. Interaction among students takes place all during the school day. One of the most important aspects of education is learning how to interact with others on the basis of the type of interdependency existing within the situation. The type of goal interdependence among individuals determines what kinds of behaviors are appropriate and effective in furthering the accomplishment of each individual's goals. Interaction among students involves three potential types of interdependence: cooperative, or positive interdependence, where students work together to accomplish shared goals; competitive, or negative interdependence, where students work against each other to achieve a goal that only one or a few students may attain; and individualistic, or no interdependence, where students work by themselves to accomplish goals that are unrelated to the goals of others.

There is an ancient story about the use of these three goal structures. Once, in a remote part of what is now the United States, there were three tribes of people who lived and hunted and did whatever it is that people do. One of the tribes had a natural inclination to compete. Whenever there was something to do, each tribesman would work anxiously to be the first one to complete the task or to do it better than anyone else. The natives competed to see who had the most comfortable cave. They competed to see who could hunt and garden best. Those who were not successful in getting food and making their caves warm and comfortable died. Eventually, the strong who survived began to compete in more dangerous ways, and people died who tried to kill the saber-toothed tiger barehanded, people died who fought over food and camping sights, and finally only one member of the tribe was left! He soon died because he did not know how to behave when he was not competing with someone else!

Another tribe had a natural inclination to do things alone. Each member hunted on his own, worked on his own cave, and preferred to be away from other people. When danger threatened, each would try to deal with it on his own. Many members of the tribe died during a great flood when each tried to build a dike around his own cave while ignoring everyone else's plight. Once many of the children were killed by a saber-toothed tiger because each tribesman ignored the situation and failed to warn others about the tiger's presence. For such reasons, the tribe did not last long. Being extreme individualists, the tribesmen did not reproduce very well, and most children did not survive very well on their own during the first year or so of their life.

◇◇

"Cooperation, not conflict, was evidently the selectively most valuable form of behavior for man taken at any stage of his evolutionary history, and surely, quite as evidently never more so than today. . . . It is essentially the experience, the means, that fits human beings not to their external environment so much as to one another. It must never be forgotten that society is fundamentally, essentially, and in all ways a cooperative enterprise, an enterprise designed to keep men in touch with one another. Without the cooperation of its members society cannot survive, and the society of man has survived because the cooperativeness of its members made survival possible—it was not an advantageous individual here and there who did so, but the group. In human societies the individuals who are most likely to survive are those who are best enabled to do so by their group."

Ashley Montagu, 1965

◇◇

The third tribe had a natural inclination to work together on the daily tasks, Some of the tribe hunted as teams: a few would drive the game toward the others so they could have easy shots at the prey. Others made warm and comfortable clothing and blankets from the skins and traded them for food. One person might make bows while his friend made arrows; together they supplied the whole tribe with hunting weapons. In fact, everyone contributed in some way to the survival of the tribe. Because each helped the other, they were a very supportive and friendly tribe and had lots of parties and fun. They developed improved ways of communicating, of coordinating their work and play, of enjoying the fruits of the world, and of developing their unique personalities. As a tribe, they survived and prospered, and it is from them that we all have descended.

This story demonstrates the fact that the most important and frequent type of interdependence among persons is cooperative. Cooperative interaction is a biological necessity for humans (Mead, 1934; Asch, 1952; Deutsch, 1962; Bruner, 1966; Johnson, 1973a). There is a deep human need to respond to others and to operate jointly with them toward mutual goals; this kind of interaction has always been absolutely necessary for the survival of every individual member of our species. No person would survive the first hour, or the first few years, of life without cooperative interaction with others, and no group or society would exist without massive cooperation among members. Without cooperation, no family, group, organization, or society could exist. This point will be further discussed in Chapter 3. Cooperative experiences are also the most essential ingredient for the development of psychological health. Cooperative interaction with others is essential for the development of trust, self-confidence, goal-setting, personal identity, and cognitive development, which are the foundation for a person's mental health (Johnson, 1974; Johnson and Matross, 1975). *No aspect of human experience is more important than cooperative interaction with others.*

The importance of cooperation does not mean that competitive and individualistic experiences should be ignored. There are times when competition is enjoyable and provides an opportunity to apply one's competencies to compare oneself with others. Acting independently is often an opportunity to experience success on one's own and to express one's autonomy. Thus every person must also have competitive and individualistic experiences and must master the skills involved in competing and working independently.

The research evidence suggests that teachers are presently overusing competition, possibly misusing the individualistic goal structure, and underusing cooperation in their classrooms. This situation will become clear in the following sections as we examine the effects each type of goal structure has upon the cognitive and affective outcomes of learning and the way in which students interact; we shall then review the appropriate use of each type of structure. In order to make this chapter more readable,

What would your ideal classroom look like? Would students be interacting, or would every student be working by himself? Would students be sharing ideas and materials and helping each other complete assignments, or would students be hiding their ideas from each other and asking only the teacher for help? Would students be studying alone or with each other? Would the teacher be the center of attention, or would students be working in groups with the teacher observing their progress? Write out a description of your ideal classroom and discuss it with two others. Then observe two classrooms and write descriptions of what they are like. Finally, compare your ideal classroom with the classrooms you observed. What are the differences? What are the similarities? How will you need to behave as a teacher to create your ideal classroom?

we have eliminated most of the references to research that support the conclusions we make. Interested readers can examine the research support for our statements by reading Appendix A.

INSTRUCTIONAL CLIMATE: INTERPERSONAL PROCESSES

Every school, classroom, and instructional group has its own climate. In one classroom, students will be having discussions, sharing materials, giving support and help to each other, communicating openly and freely, and involving themselves in instructional activities; in another classroom, students will be working by themselves, ignoring other students, avoiding communication, hiding materials from each other, and withdrawing from instructional activities. These patterns of interaction among students are the climate of the classroom, and that climate will have a large impact upon the behavior of students and the amount of learning that takes place (Johnson, 1970). *The classroom climate consists of the ways in which the people within the classroom interact with each other.* Each type of goal structure will promote a different pattern of interaction among students; that is, a different learning climate. Interpersonal processes important for learning are:

> interaction among students
> mutual liking
> effective communication
> trust
> acceptance and support
> utilization of personal resources
> sharing and helping

emotional involvement
coordination of effort
division of labor
divergent and risk-taking thinking

A summary of the research findings on the use of cooperative, individualistic, and competitive goal structures is presented in Table 2-1.

TABLE 2-1
Goal Structures and Interpersonal Processes

Cooperative	Competitive	Individualistic
High interaction	Low interaction	No interaction
Mutual liking	Mutual dislike	No interaction
Effective communication	No communication or misleading communication	No interaction
High trust	Low trust	No interaction
High mutual influence	Low mutual influence	No interaction
High acceptance and support	Low acceptance and support	No interaction
High utilization of resources of other students	No utilization of resources of other students	No interaction
High sharing and helping	Attempts to mislead and obstruct others	No interaction
High emotional involvement of all students	Emotional involvement of some students (winners)	No interaction
High coordination of effort	Low coordination of effort	No interaction
Division of labor possible	Division of labor not possible	No interaction
High divergent and risk-taking thinking	Low divergent and risk-taking thinking	No interaction
No comparison of self versus others	High comparison of self versus others	No interaction

Does this table seem reasonable? Think about it. Cooperation by its very nature provides opportunities for positive interaction among students, while competition promotes cautious and defensive interaction (except under very limited conditions). When students are in an individualistic goal structure, they need to be left alone to master the skill or knowledge and would only be obstructed and distracted by interaction with other students. The individualistic goal structure, however, will promote more interaction between each student and the teacher. Thus, if the teacher wishes to promote positive interaction among students, cooperative goal structures should be used, and individualistic and competitive goal structures should be avoided in most cases. Cooperative goal structures will promote interpersonal processes that will generally improve the quality of classroom life and increase the enjoyment and productiveness of both the teacher and the students. The more students like each other, the more they communicate effectively with each other; the higher the trust, influence, acceptance, support, sharing, helping, emotional involvement, and utilization of each other's resources, the more the coordination of effort; and the more the divergent and risk-taking thinking, the more learning takes place, and the more positive are the affective and cognitive outcomes of instruction.

Teaching question: "How do I increase trust, liking, friendliness, helping, communication, and involvement among my students, while reducing the amount of student-student conflict and disruption, all with little effort on my part?"

Research answer: Structure cooperative situations.

STUDENTS ARE MOTIVATED TO ACHIEVE LEARNING GOALS
WITHIN GOAL STRUCTURES
THAT AFFECT
INTERPERSONAL, GROUP, AND CLASSROOM PROCESSES
AND
COGNITIVE AND AFFECTIVE OUTCOMES

OUTCOMES OF INSTRUCTION

All teaching is aimed at promoting cognitive and affective development and change in students. All instruction has anticipated and unanticipated consequences. Teachers regularly plan activities to accomplish their objectives by changing students (teaching students how to read is an example of such a change). The types of outcomes planned for are diverse and depend upon the age of the students and the nature of the instructional units. There are long-term outcomes sought for the school as a whole, and there are short-term outcomes sought through daily instructional activities. In this section we shall first mention briefly some of the long-term outcomes and then discuss more specific cognitive and affective short-term outcomes.

What are the desired long-term outcomes of schooling? What is it that schools work to achieve in student development? The overall purpose of schools is to develop each student to maximum capacity as a productive and self-actualizing member of society. Students should therefore be taught the values, habits, knowledge, attitudes, and skills needed to fill specific adult roles and to live a fulfilling, satisfying life in a complex, democratic, industrial society. They should develop the capacity for "role-responsibility" (i.e., the capacity to live up to general expectations of appropriate role behavior, such as promptness and cleanliness) and "role readiness" (i.e., the ability to meet the demands of many organizational settings with the proper cooperation); they should commit themselves to occupational roles, become "self-actualizing" (i.e., develop their personal potentials, resources, and abilities and utilize them in living a fulfilling life), have enough personal flexibility to live in a rapidly changing world, and enjoy healthy physical and psychological development.

Traditionally, schools have focused upon priorities that are verbal-conceptual in nature, but increased recognition of the necessity to include affective aspects of learning in formulating goals is changing the nature of instruction. Whereas in the past, educators have concentrated on producing students who can deal with the words, concepts, and mathematical symbols so necessary for success in our technological society, they are now becoming concerned with the attitudes and values that students develop. Every learning experience has both cognitive and affective outcomes. *Affective* refers to the feeling or emotional aspect of experiencing and learning, and *cognitive* refers to the intellectual or conceptual activity in experiencing and learning. It should be emphasized that a person's affect and cognitions cannot be separated. For each cognitive response, there are changes in affect; to teach any concept, principle, or theory is to teach not only its comprehension but also for an attitude toward it. A school, for example, wants not only to teach a student to read but also wants the student to enjoy, appreciate, and value reading. On the other hand, each affective response to instruction has a cognitive counterpart. In order for a student to be aware of her feelings, she has to conceptualize the feeling and place it in the context of the situation she is experiencing; at the very least, this calls for cognitions about one's feelings, and generally it means that there is a cognitive component of being aware of and experiencing a feeling or an emotion. We have separated the inseparable for the purpose of clarity in presenting outcomes in this chapter, realizing that every experience has a cognition component (what you do during and can say after the experience) and an affective component (how you feel during and after the experience).

The fundamental facts that brought about cooperation, society, and civilization and transformed the animal man into a human being are the facts that work performed under the division of labor is more productive than isolated work and that man's reason is capable of recognizing this truth. But for these facts men would have forever remained deadly foes of one another, irreconcilable rivals in their endeavors to secure a portion of the scarce supply of means of sustenance provided by Nature. Each man would have been forced to view all other men as his enemies; his craving for the satisfaction of his own appetites would have brought him into an implacable conflict with all his neighbors. No sympathy could possibly develop under such a state of affairs. . . . We may call consciousness of kind, sense of community, or sense of belonging together the acknowledgement of fact that all other human beings are potential collaborators in the struggle for survival because they are capable of recognizing the mutual benefits of cooperation. . . .

Ludwig Von Mises, 1949

COGNITIVE OUTCOMES

What are the specific cognitive outcomes schools are concerned with? What cognitive outcomes should teachers promote and try to influence through instructional programs? Certainly the mastery of basic facts, concepts, principles, and skills is often emphasized. The development of verbal abilities, to be able to communicate information effectively through speaking, writing, and reading, is a traditional emphasis. Perhaps equally important is the teaching of the cooperative problem-solving skills needed to develop and revise knowledge, since most of the information and theories learned in elementary school will be untrue, irrelevant, or dramatically changed by the time students enter college. Cooperative problem-solving skills are also essential for the retention, application, and transfer of factual information, concepts, and principles. The cooperative skills of joining with other individuals to accomplish a common task or solve a common problem is one of the most important cognitive outcomes of schooling. No effective problem solving can take place without some amount of creativity. Creativity is not a characteristic of a person but rather the result of certain types of interaction among individuals (Johnson and Johnson, 1975). The ability to engage in divergent thinking, to take risks in solving problems, and to engage in open controversy are all aspects of creative interaction. The ability to identify one's abilities and apply them in problem-solving situations is an important cognitive outcome. The quantity and speed of work on simple drill activities can be considered a cognitive outcome. Finally, the development of the ability to take the perspective of other individuals within a situation is a necessary prerequisite for the development of social adjustment, communication ability and skills, empathy and sympathy, and autonomous moral judgment based upon mutual reciprocity and justice (Johnson, 1974a). It is, therefore, an important cognitive skill.

Table 2-2 summarizes the relationship between goal structures and cognitive outcomes of instruction. Research indicates that the following types of outcomes will be facilitated by cooperative goal structures (see Appendix A). When the instructional task is some sort of problem-solving activity, a cooperative goal structure clearly results in higher achievement than does a competitive or an individualistic goal structure. There is evidence that factual material will be remembered better if it is discussed in a cooperatively structured group. Cooperative goal structures also facilitate mastery of concepts and principles and of creative processes (such as divergent thinking, risk-taking thinking, and entering into controversy). They are effective in developing verbal and problem-solving skills, cooperative skills, and the ability to see a situation from someone else's perspective

TABLE 2-2
Goal Structures and Cognitive Outcomes

Cognitive Outcome	Cooperative	Competitive	Individualistic
Mastery of factual information			x
Retention, application, and transfer of factual information, concepts, principles	x		
Mastery of concepts and principles	x		
Verbal abilities	x		
Problem-solving ability and success	x		
Cooperative skills	x		
Creative ability: divergent and risk-taking thinking, productive controversy	x		
Awareness and utilization of one's capabilities	x		
Perspective- (role-) taking abilities	x		
Speed and quantity of work on simple drill activities		x	
Competitive skills		x	
Individualistic skills			x
Simple mechanical skills			x

(an ability that is essential to empathy, social adjustment, communication, and autonomous moral judgment). In turn, the development of cooperative skills is essential to a person's self-actualization, i.e., the development of one's potentialities and the utilization of those potentialities.

What are the types of cognitive outcomes facilitated by individualistic goal structures? Generally, specific information within subject areas can be learned better through individualistic procedures—programmed learning or other master techniques. This information would include appropriate terminology or background information that might also be useful in other situations. Simple skills like spelling, specific procedures for organizing material, the use of a microscope, are also appropriately taught individually. Some individualistic skills, such as monitoring self-progress, working by oneself, and organizing one's time and effort, are best learned under this goal structure. For the knowledge or skills gained to be retained

and transferred appropriately to other situations, however, they need to be applied in problem-solving situations under a cooperative goal structure.

What are the types of cognitive instructional objectives facilitated by competitive goal structures? A competitive goal structure is effective in increasing performance on simple drill activities and on speed-related tasks where sheer quantity of work is desired on a project that requires little help from other persons. Competition provides appropriate practice for some of the skills learned in an individualistic or cooperative setting, and a "game" format is often used. Reading and language games, math facts and calculation speed, athletic contests, and puzzles are examples of such tasks. Competitive skills, which include knowing how to be a good winner or loser, how to compare one's performance with that of other students, and how to obstruct the performance of others, are learned in a competitive situation.

AFFECTIVE OUTCOMES

Since emotional responses affect the amount of energy available for learning, the personal importance of learning to the students, and the degree to which students will apply and utilize their learning in the future, affective responses are of extreme importance to the teacher. If schools are to be successful in influencing a person long after he has completed school or during the hours when he is not in school, the development of positive affective responses toward the material and skills learned is an important emphasis. The *affective outcomes* of education are the feelings, attitudes, and values the school promotes as part of the instructional program (Johnson, 1973b, 1974b; Watson and Johnson, 1972). An *attitude* is a response —favorable or unfavorable—toward a particular person, object, or experience. It has cognitive (perception of the object, experience, or person), affective (feelings of positiveness or negativeness), and behavioral (actions taken) components. A *value* exists whenever an emotion implying liking or disliking attaches to a cognition; values express a relationship between a person's emotional feelings and particular cognitive catergories. When a person declares, "Stealing is wrong" she is expressing a value by attaching a feeling (wrongness) to a category (stealing). Anything that one approaches, desires, or espouses reflects a positive value, while anything he avoids, dislikes, or deplores reflects a negative value. Both attitudes and values imply what behavior is appropriate when confronted with a particular person, object, or experience. Traditionally, attitudes and values have been differentiated, despite their common qualities and similarities. For one thing, persons hold many more attitudes than values; an adult probably has hundreds of attitudes but only dozens of values. A cluster of attitudes surrounds a value; for any given value, a number of attitudes can be expressed.

What are the specific affective outcomes schools are concerned with? Several noted social scientists have stated that the most pressing need in our society of organized complexity and constant change is for persons who are skilled in being human; that is, for persons who can feel and express warmth, trust, caring, openness, compassion, altruism, and other aspects of "humanness." Thus one set of important affective outcomes are the feelings, attitudes, and values necessary for humane interaction among students, including the interpersonal and group skills needed to form and maintain humanizing relationships. A full discussion of humanistic relationships is presented in Johnson (1973a), and the specific interpersonal and group skills needed for humanistic interaction are presented in Johnson (1972) and Johnson and Johnson (1975). Other areas of affective outcomes include: valuing a pluralistic, democratic society within which there is freedom of choice and equality of opportunity; promoting the acceptance and appreciation of cultural, ethnic, and individual differences and a reduction of prejudice and bias; acquiring values relating to the importance and utility of education and the free and open inquiry into all problems; positive attitudes toward school, subject areas, instructional activities, school personnel, and other students; accepting learning as a source of excitement, interest, enjoyment, and satisfaction; the absence of high levels of anxiety over long periods of time; the perception and attitudes of oneself as valuable, acceptable, competent, and able to affect one's life; psychological health; and finally, the development of the capacity for feeling a variety of emotions at wide levels of intensity.

TABLE 2-3
Goal Structures and Affective Outcomes

Affective Outcomes	Cooperative	Competitive	Individualistic
Interpersonal skills for "humanness"	x		
Group skills for "humanness"	x		
Pluralistic, democratic values	x		
Acceptance and appreciation of cultural, ethnic, and individual differences	x		
Reduction of prejudice and bias	x		
Valuing education	x		
Positive attitudes toward school, subject area, instructional activities, school personnel, and other students	x		
Enjoyment and satisfaction from learning	x		
Moderate levels of anxiety to promote learning	x		
Positive self attitudes	x		
Emotional capacity	x		

Considerable research has been done on the effects of goal structures on the affective outcomes of instruction. As can be seen from Table 2-3, affective outcomes, similar to interpersonal processes, are promoted primarily by cooperative goal structures. Cooperative interaction promotes the interpersonal and group skills needed for humanizing interaction; the problem solving promoted by cooperative goal structures and the democratic biases contained in cooperation foster the development of democratic values. Cooperative goal structures promote appreciation for cultural, ethnic, and individual differences because heterogeneity improves the functioning of a problem-solving group. Membership in cooperatively structured groups formed to accomplish instructional objectives has been found to reduce prejudice and bias among members of different racial groups. Through a division of labor and a shared responsibility for goal accomplishment, every member's resources are utilized in a cooperative group and, therefore, are valued in helping the group accomplish its learning goals. Through promoting the use and application of knowledge for problem-solving purposes, the value of education is emphasized in cooperative learning groups. There is evidence that students have more positive attitudes toward school, subject areas, instructional activities, teachers, other school personnel, and other students under a cooperative goal structure. When given a choice, students choose cooperative over competitive and individualistic goal structures. The amount of failure experienced by students within a cooperative goal structure is less than that experienced by students within a competitive goal structure. Participation in a joint effort to accomplish learning goals produces an enjoyment and satisfaction that promotes successful instruction. The level of anxiety that students experience in a cooperative situation is less than that experienced by students in a competitive situation. Positive self-attitudes of being valuable, acceptable, competent, and able to influence one's world are all promoted by cooperative goal structures. As more openness, communication, feedback, and interaction are promoted by cooperation, the student's emotional capacity is enlarged. Finally, cooperative attitudes and values are learned in cooperative goal structures.

What are the affective outcomes promoted by individualistic goal structures? Since no interaction with other students is promoted under this goal structure, the possibility of positive affective outcomes is minimized. The accomplishment of successful mastery of material may produce satisfaction. Students interviewed by the authors have reported feelings of loneliness, isolation, alienation, and not getting enough time from the teacher when working on individualistically structured activities for long periods of time. Such feelings do not promote positive attitudes toward education and schooling. It might be noted, however, that many of the programs now called individualized education are more cooperatively than individualistically structured.

What are the affective outcomes promoted by competitive goal structures? When used under the appropriate conditions and when used as a change of pace rather than as a continual goal structure, competition can be fun, exciting, and a potential for release of energy and aggressive feelings. In general, however, competition, when used inappropriately or too frequently, results in a variety of very negative affective outcomes that will be discussed in the next chapter.

Value of Cooperative Goal Structures

There are at least three reasons why cooperative goal structures are valuable for a classroom teacher. The first reason is that cooperative goal structures are easier to set up, monitor, and evaluate in terms of teaching time and effort than are individualistic or competitive goal structures. This point will be discussed further in Chapters 8 and 9, but it can be stated here that in competitive and individualized situations the teacher must be the major source of help and support for each student, while in a cooperative situation the students receive help and support from each other.

The second reason, that cooperative goal structures promote helping and sharing among students, has several advantages:

1. Peer tutors are often effective in teaching children who do not respond well to adults.
2. Peer tutoring can develop a deep bond of friendship between the tutor and the person being helped, the result of which is very important for integrating slow learners into the group.
3. Peer tutoring takes pressure off the teacher by allowing her to teach a large group of students; at the same time, it allows the slow learners the individual attention they need.
4. The tutors benefit by learning to teach, a general skill that can be very useful in an adult society.
5. Peer tutoring happens spontaneously under cooperative conditions, so the teacher does not have to organize and manage it in a formal, continuing way.

The third reason is that cooperation promotes the type of learning climate and the cognitive and affective outcomes that make teaching more effective and more fun.

It should be noted that just because a teacher structures a learning situation cooperatively it does not follow that students will always behave cooperatively. A student must have the skills necessary for cooperative behavior and must make a decision to use them. Skills are needed by students to function in the other two goal structures as well. This issue will be discussed more thoroughly in the following chapters, especially in Chapter 6.

"man is a mythmaking animal
who prefers
to embrace the myths
that keep him comfortable
rather than inquire
into the facts
that enjoin him to think"
Montagu

THREE

Reexamination of the use of cooperative, competitive, and individualistic goal structures

INTRODUCTION

Once a child enters the first grade, there is great concern about whether his performance is equal or superior to other children his age. Across the country, students are regularly compared to see who is superior and who is inferior. The competitive goal structure so pervades American education that it is sometimes difficult to see how we can get along without it. Most of us, teachers and students alike, don't realize how deeply embedded this goal structure is in our daily school routines. At the present time the chief competitor of the competitive goal structure is individualized instruction. Behavior modification, teaching machines, and dissatisfaction with competition have all led to the advocacy of individualistic goal structures. Yet it is cooperation that is most productive in creating fruitful learning climates and in promoting the accomplishment of most cognitive and affective outcomes. In this chapter we shall examine the myths and criticisms connected with each of the three goal structures. We shall first discuss the undesirable outcomes of inappropriate competition and then review the myths that support its use. Discussions of individualized and cooperative instruction will follow.

WHAT ARE THE UNDESIRABLE OUTCOMES OF COMPETITION?

Competition as a goal structure did not emerge with a very positive image in the last chapter, and it fares even worse in the research review in Appendix A. The specific undesirable outcomes of the inappropriate use and overuse of competition are considerable.

In the traditional competitive classroom the purpose of evaluation is to rank students from the "best" to the "worst." Even if teachers don't use scores and performances in this way, the students tend to rank their fellow students. In most classrooms, fairly stable patterns of achievement exist so that the majority of students always "lose" and a few students always "win." Thus a student may spend twelve years in public schools being confronted daily with the fact that he is a "loser." Although there is no experimental research on the effects of prolonged failure experiences, it seems reasonable to assume that the student's self-attitudes and feelings of competence will be affected. If the student desires to "win," the daily frustration of "losing" may result in a sense of worthlessness, helplessness, and incompetence.

◇◇

Only a few children in school ever become good at learning in the way we try to make them learn. Most of them get humiliated, frightened, and discouraged. They use their minds, not to learn, but to get out of doing the things we tell them to do—to make them learn. In the short run, these strategies seem to work. They make it possible for many children to get through their schooling even though they learn very little. But in the long run these strategies are self-limiting and self-defeating, and destroy both character and intelligence. The children who use such strategies are prevented by them from growing into more than limited versions of the human beings they might have become. This is the real failure that takes place in school; hardly any children escape.

John Holt, *How Children Learn*

◇◇

Hurlock (1972) found in an experiment with children that members of a group that was defeated on the first of four days of competition never overcame their initial failure and attained inferior scores for the entire duration of the experiment, even though the groups had been matched on the basis of ability. Tseng (1969) found that as rewards increase in value, so do the tension and frustration of failure; children who failed in competitive situations performed poorly in subsequent competitions. Atkinson (1965) would predict from his theory of achievement motivation that the student who chronically experiences failure will become primarily oriented toward avoiding failure (thus becoming nonachievement oriented). The tendency to avoid failure inhibits the student from attempting a task on which he is to be evaluated, especially when the probability of success is intermediate. Students, however, are forced into achievement-oriented situations. In such a case the student who is dominated by a tendency to avoid failure is likely to choose tasks with a very high or a very low chance of success. Doing so minimizes his anxiety about failure, for if the chance of success is very high, he is almost sure not to fail, and when the chance for success is very low, no one can blame him for failure.

◇◇

Is competition ever valuable? Are there any conditions under which a teacher would want to use interpersonal competition? We have already emphasized that all three goal structures have their place and should be used. In Chapter 4, we shall detail the conditions under which interpersonal competition can be used to promote student learning and to increase student enjoyment of learning. It is the present inappropriate and overuse of competition that is being referred to in the discussion of destructive outcomes.

◇◇

A large number of educators, psychologists, and popular writers have challenged the notion that it is an inevitable part of American education for a large proportion of students to experience failure (Silberman, 1971; Glasser, 1969; Wilhelms, 1970; Kagan, 1965; Holt, 1964; Jackson, 1968; Illich, 1971; Postman and Weingartner, 1969; Kohl, 1969; Nesbitt, 1967; Rogers, 1970; Walberg and Thomas, 1971; Rathbone, 1970). Holt (1969) states that for the student the most interesting thing in the classroom is the other students, but in a competitive goal structure the student must ignore them, act as if these other students, all about him, only a few feet away, are really not there. He cannot interact with them, talk with them, smile at them—often he cannot even look at them. In many schools he cannot talk to other students in the halls between classes; in many schools he cannot talk to other students during lunch. Holt states that this is splendid training for a world in which, when you are not studying the other person to figure out how to do him in, you pay no attention to him.

One probable and undesirable affective outcome of a pervasive competitive situation is that individuals will try to obstruct each other's goal accomplishment, and they will dislike behaviors that facilitate another person's goal accomplishment. They will have hostile and angry feelings toward individuals who "win," thus relegating them to failure, or will become angry at the teacher, at the school, or at themselves (expressed in such ways as depression, self-punishment, withdrawal, or self-destructiveness). Kagan (1965) notes that individuals who are vulnerable to guilt over hostile thoughts and feelings toward others may become anxious when placed in a competitive structure and therefore inhibited in their competitiveness, which reduces their chances for success. Furthermore, students who are sensitive to their peers' rejection may fear the consequences of winning and thus not achieve up to their potential.

Even when a student is one of the few individuals who experience success most of the time, an emphasis upon competition can have long-term destructive consequences. If a student is continually reinforced and given attention and approval for "winning," he may believe that a person is valued only for his "wins" and not for himself. The result of this belief is a need to prove continually his value, through achievement. There is a basic rejection of the student as a person in such a process.

One of the most interesting discussions of the destructiveness of competition is by Bertrand Russell (1930). He notes that the "rat race" in American life does not have its origin in people's fears that they will fail to get their breakfast the next morning, but rather that they will fail to outshine their neighbors. The lives of many individuals seem to have the psychology of the 100-yard dash, and they remain too anxious and concentrate too much upon "winning" to be happy. All the quieter pleasures become abandoned. Russell sees such an emphasis upon competition as a general decay of civilized standards. He believes that the competitive philosophy of life, which views life as a contest in which respect is to be accorded to the victor, breeds a dinosaur cycle, where intelligence is ignored for strength and finally where the powerful (but stupid) kill each other off, leaving the world for the intelligent bystanders. Being sterile due to high anxiety over success is an example of such selective evolution. Russell states:

> Competition considered as the main thing in life is too grim, too tenacious, too much a matter of taut muscles and intent will, to make a possible basis of life for more than one or two generations at most. After that length of time it must produce nervous fatigue, various phenomena of escape, a pursuit of pleasure as tense and as difficult as work (since relaxing has become impossible), and in the end a disappearance of the stock through sterility. It is not only work that is poisoned by the philosophy of competition; leisure is poisoned just as much. The kind of leisure which is quiet and restoring to the nerves comes to be felt boring. There is bound to be a continual acceleration of which the natural termination would be drugs and collapse. The cure for this lies in admitting the part of sane and quiet enjoyment in a balanced ideal of life. [p. 34].

For the teacher who is truly interested in intellectual functioning, one of the saddest probable consequences of the continual use of competitive goal structures is that the intrinsic motivation for learning and thinking will become subverted. A highly competitive person does not learn for intrinsic reasons; learning is a means to an end, the end being "winning." Intellectual pursuit for itself becomes unheard of; knowledge that does not help one "win" becomes a waste of time. Thus Leonard (1968) states that when learning becomes truly rewarding for its own sake, competition will be seen to be irrelevant to the learning process and damaging to the development of free-ranging, lifelong learners. Neill (1960) states that to get the better of another person is "a damnable objective"; he believes that when the child's natural interest in things is considered, one begins to realize the destructiveness of competition for rewards or for the avoidance of punishments. For Neill, true interest is the life force of the whole personality, and such interest is completely spontaneous and cannot be compelled through competitive goal structures.

In the review of research in Appendix A, it is possible to note a variety of undesirable cognitive and affective outcomes of competition in comparison with cooperation. Students will be dissatisfied if they are not winning and will dislike any behavior or event that helps another person to win; ultimately, they will dislike the students who are successful. Competitive situations are characterized by either the absence of communication or misleading communication, distrustful and negative attitudes toward each other, frequent misperceptions about each other's behavior, and a tendency to define conflicts as "win-lose" situations. In a competitive situation, differences in behavior and background are often perceived as threatening as they may provide others with some advantage in accomplishing the goal; differences that reduce the chances of others to "win" will be ridiculed and looked down upon. Prejudice and discrimination against minority groups increase and are perpetuated under competitive conditions. There is more apathy toward learning and negative attitudes toward school, teachers, education, and subject areas. Anxiety is often high in competitive situations. Achievement in problem-solving situations will be low. When competition is overused or used inappropriately, the negative cognitive and affective outcomes are staggering and overwhelming. There can be no doubt that the pervasive use of interpersonal competition leads to dehumanization among students and to the sabotaging of the instructional program.

MYTHS SUPPORTING THE USE OF COMPETITION

With all these negative outcomes resulting from the use of competition, why then has it been so prevalent for so many years? The answer lies in the nature of myths about effective teaching. When trying to teach certain principles, a teacher will engage in behavior which she believes will effectively accomplish her teaching goals. What a teacher does in the classroom is based upon what she believes will be effective. When asked why she is teaching in certain ways, the teacher will state her beliefs as to what constitutes effective teaching. Beliefs both guide practice and provide the justification and rationale for practice. Thus, all the teacher's behaviors in conducting instructional activities are based upon beliefs. When a teaching practice has been used for several years, it becomes a tradition. Traditions are supported by beliefs and assumptions about their benefits and effectiveness. Many teacher beliefs and traditions are passed down from one generation of teachers to another (through curriculum, advice giving, modelling, and teacher educators) with very little evidence to back up their validity. Sometimes these beliefs are valid, and other times they are fictitious. A fictitious belief or assumption is a *myth*! When teaching is based upon myths, ineffective instruction results.

Myths are interesting things. Sometimes they generate great fascination and efforts to make them come true, as did, for instance, the search for the fountain of youth. Sometimes they are entertaining, such as the myths of unicorns and great past heros. Sometimes they result in physical pain, such as the myth believed by the younger of the two authors that he was equal to the older of the two authors while growing up. Some myths are harmless, but others, like the myth that interpersonal competition always facilitates learning, are destructive.

Like most myths aimed at justifying current practices, the myths surrounding competition came about when attempts were made to explain why students were ranked in terms of their ability to perform educational tasks. The explanations for the use of interpersonal competition range from "preparation for a dog-eat-dog, survival of the fittest world" to "increased motivation to perform at the utmost of one's abilities." Since teachers are held accountable for what takes place within the classroom (although they often have little choice about what happens there), they are often the ones who most vehemently defend the status quo of interpersonal competition. Teachers who use interpersonal competition are likely to say that it motivates students, increases learning, improves character, and trains students to do well in a competitive society. In the following paragraphs we shall examine each of these myths about competition.

© 1965 by United Feature Service, Inc.

MYTH 1: Our society is highly competitive and students must be educated to succeed in a "survival of the fittest" world.

The popular version of Darwin's theory of evolution states that only the fittest survive and that only through succeeding in extreme competition can a person be born in a log cabin but become president of the United States. Many advocates of competition insist that schools must emphasize a dog-eat-dog theory of survival in the occupational world. To be better than the Joneses is the deepest desire of such individuals. Yet the truth is that the vast majority of human interaction, in our society as well as in all other societies, is not competitive, but cooperative. We are a social species. Cooperation is a biological necessity for humans (Mead, 1934; Asch, 1952; Deutsch, 1962; Bruner, 1966; Johnson, 1973a). Without cooperation among persons, no group, no family, no organization, and no school would be able to exist. Without high levels of cooperation there would be no coordination of behavior on highways or sidewalks, in stores, within organizations, or anywhere else. This book would not have been written, published, or read without cooperation! No two individuals could communicate with each other or interact without cooperating to form a common language and agreed-upon norms for behavior. Societies would not exist, exchange of goods and services would not take place, entertainment would not be possible, occupations would not be available, education would be unheard of—complete anarchy would exist without cooperation.

"All of us are the inheritors of a tradition of thought, relating to the nature of life, which has been handed down to us from the nineteenth century. Life, this view holds, is struggle, competition, the survival of the fittest. In the jungle, a fight with 'Nature, red in tooth and claw'; in society, the claw is perhaps gloved, and the fight is called a 'struggle' in which 'the race is to the swiftest,' in which 'the strongest survive and the weakest go to the wall.' "

Montagu, 1966

"All plants and animals are bound together by sharing the same earth, air, and water. They are also linked by a competition for solar energy, on which their lives depend. Once believed to be a ruthless and unbridled battle, more recent study of this struggle for existence suggests that cooperation and interdepedence may be more important for the survival of a species than a no-quarter war."

Peter Farb, *Ecology*

Even in fighting wars and conducting competitive activities, there are vast underpinnings of cooperative agreements concerning how the competition or conflict will be conducted and the ways in which antagonists can express their hostility toward each other. There can be no competition without underlying cooperation. A study of social psychology suggests that competition is a very, very small part of interacting with other individuals in our society and probably not a very important type of human interaction.

MYTH 2: *Achievement, success, outstanding performance, superhuman effort, the rise of the great leader, drive, ambition, and motivation depend upon competing with others.*

The appeal of this myth to persons who wish to see greatness is overwhelming. Where is the great person who will set the world straight and show us a better way of life? How else do the great hunters, the presidents of huge organizations, the self-made millionaires, the religious prophets, and the outstanding statesmen achieve their greatness? The actual results of the research studies, however, burst this balloon. Higher achievement does not take place within a competitive goal structure; in fact, it is cooperation that facilitates high achievement. Quality of performance goes down under competitive goal structures, and a person who is superior in one situation may be markedly inferior in another. The use of competition will, under most conditions, decrease the quality of a student's work and will in no way determine who is the best person to achieve under a variety of conditions. Nelson and Kagan (1972) note that competitive motivation interferes with one's capacity for the adaptive problem solving necessary in dealing with complex issues with others. Achievement motivation theory, furthermore, emphasizes the challenge of moderate risks of failure in increasing competence, and such a process is based upon one's assessment of the difficulty of the task and one's present ability level, not upon being better than others. Just as failing to achieve a goal does not mean losing to others, success in achieving a goal does not depend upon winning over others; cooperative groups can succeed or fail at task accomplishment just as competitive individuals can. Finally, competition does not motivate many students. The only students who are motivated by competition are those who believe they have a good chance of winning. Persons do not exert effort to achieve the impossible. Competition is threatening and discouraging to those who believe they cannot win, and many students will withdraw psychologically or physically or only half try in competitive situations. Students are motivated when a goal is desirable, possible, challenging, concrete, and requires positive interaction with other students. A competitive goal structure does not affect any of these variables in a positive way unless the student believes he has an equal chance of winning. The whole area of intrinsic motivation shows that motivation does not depend upon competition. Even in extrinsic motivation situations, competition will exist only when there is a limited amount of the reinforcer (it cannot be shared with everyone), and when every student believes he has a chance to win.

◇◇

"There is nothing new in all this. We have heard it before. During the latter half of the 19th century, and during the early part of the 20th century, this viewpoint formed the foundation for the doctrine of 'Social Darwinism.' It was implied in such ideas as 'The Survival of the Fittest' and 'The Struggle for Existence,' and in such phrases as 'The Weakest Go To The Wall,' 'Competition is the Life-Blood of a Nation,' and the like. Such ideas were not merely taken to explain, but were actually used to justify violence and war."

Ashley Montagu, 1965

◇◇

MYTH 3: *Competition builds character and toughens the young for life in the real world.*

Underneath each competitive athletic program is the belief that competition builds character. If one competes on the football field, one builds the character to win in congress! Ogilvie and Tutko (1971) spent eight years studying the effects of competition on the personality. They focused upon athletic competition, as "a young athlete often must face in hours or days the kind of pressure that occurs in the life of the achievement-oriented man over several years." They found no evidence that competition in athletics builds character; indeed, they state that there is evidence that athletic competition limits growth in some areas. It is possible, they say, that competition doesn't even require much more than a minimally integrated personality. Most athletes have a low interest in receiving support and concern from others, a low need to take care of others, and a low need for affiliation with others. Research indicates that the personality of the ideal athlete is not the result of any molding process of participating in competition but rather comes out of the ruthless selection process that occurs at all levels of sport. Ogilvie and Tutko also note that competition does not toughen an individual to face other competitive situations but rather that, under the intense pressure of athletics, personality flaws manifest themselves quickly and prevent successful participation. There is, therefore, no evidence that competition builds character and toughens the individual for success in future competition; on the contrary, there is evidence that competition does just the opposite.

MYTH 4: Students prefer competitive situations.

How easy it is to believe that competition is used in schools because students demand it! Greenberg (1932) did find that children seem to enjoy competitive reward structures as long as they are winning and as long as they can exhibit some mastery of the task, but he also found that they absolutely refuse to participate in competition on several tasks. A series of more recent studies have shown that students prefer cooperatively structured instructional situations to competitive ones, especially if they have had experience in cooperative learning situations (DeVries and Edwards, 1972b; R. T. Johnson, Johnson and Bryant, 1973; R. T. Johnson, 1974; D. W. Johnson, 1973). In the Johnson, Johnson, and Bryant study, sixth grade boys were shown pictures of cooperative and competitive classroom activities; 70 percent of the boys perceived their classrooms as being competitively structured, while 66 percent indicated they would prefer a cooperative classroom. In the R. T. Johnson study, 100 percent of the sixth grade boys and girls who participated in a cooperatively structured science unit stated they preferred a cooperative classroom structure.

"Be content with your lot; one cannot be first in everything."

Aesop

"No man lives without jostling and being jostled; in all ways he has to elbow himself through the world, giving and receiving offence."

Thomas Carlyle

"You can't make the world all planned and soft. The strongest and best survive—that's the law of nature after all—always has been and always will be."

Businessman in Middletown, Lynd and Lynd

"There's no gap so large as the gap between being 'first' and being 'second.' "

Anonymous second place finisher

"It's not whether you win or lose, it's how you play the game."

Unknown

"The enjoyment of competing, win or lose, encourages competition; having to win each time discourages it."

Anonymous competitor

"A good answer may not be good enough. It has to be better than someone else's."

Dreeken in *On What Is Learned in School*

MYTH 5: Competition builds self-confidence and self-esteem.

The winner must be full of self-confidence and be proud! Yet if that is true, why do so many winners have psychological problems, especially in adapting to situations in which winning is no longer relevant? The truth seems to be that competition often leads to insecurity and negative self-attitudes (the unforgivable sin is finishing second), and most students in most classrooms experience failure most of the time under a competitive goal structure. It is impossible to make all students winners.

SHOULD COMPETITION EVER BE USED IN THE SCHOOLS?

The inappropriate use and overuse of competition (due in part to a series of myths passed down from one generation of teachers to the next) have many destructive outcomes, * which interfere seriously with successful instruction. The authors, however, do not want to leave the impression that interpersonal competition is inherently evil and should never be used for instructional purposes. Under the appropriate circumstances, competition can be exciting and enjoyable, whether the participants win or lose. Students need to learn how to recognize these circumstances and gain the perspective necessary to engage in competition successfully. The destructive effects of competition are especially marked when the specific goal structure is not made clear and a general but ambiguous competitive atmosphere is created for learning. When competition is used appropriately, there are positive benefits. In the next chapter the authors will specify the conditions under which competition should be used, and in Chapter 5 the procedures for concretely structuring competition will be detailed.

MYTHS SUPPORTING THE USE OF INDIVIDUALISTIC GOAL STRUCTURES

Because of the popular criticism of competition and the dissatisfaction of teachers with the destructive effects of overusing competition, individualized instruction has been presented as the alternative. Programmed learning, contracting, mastery programs, and tutorial programs are all presented as

---

* The effects of competing with his older brother have left one of the authors (who will remain unnamed) a broken and shattered man who wanders the streets at night with a frown on his face and a tear in his eye and a fantasy in his head that his older brother (who will also remain unnamed) is happily having a party!

the only resource?

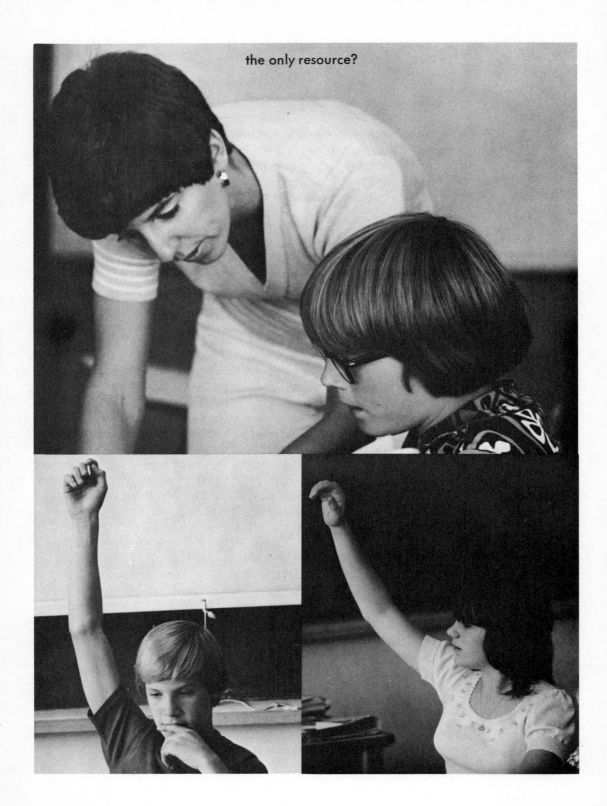

ways of individualizing instruction. Like all other education practices, there are beliefs and claims that support its use. Some of these beliefs are myths.

MYTH 1: Individualized instruction is a feasible alternative to competition as a dominant goal structure.

Because it seems the only alternative, individualized instruction has often been presented as the best alternative to competition. Yet a fully individualized instructional program may be impossible if a teacher has more than one student. In the pure sense, individualized instruction means providing every student with a unique and personalized set of learning experiences, including: (1) an extensive diagnosis of the student's aptitude, achievement, interests, learning styles, and other qualities having implications for the planning of education programs, (2) individual objectives, (3) an individualistic goal structure, (4) the placing of each student at the point in the curriculum appropriate to his current knowledge and skills, (5) an individual set of resources and materials appropriately matched to the student's aptitude, previous achievements, interests, and learning style, (6) an expected rate and amount of learning appropriate to the person, (7) an individualized procedure for obtaining extensive information concerning student progress, and (8) a method of individualized evaluation and feedback. This approach would require so much work from the teacher that it seems impossible to implement as a total, or even major, approach to teaching.

MYTH 2: Students work on their own and need little or no assistance from the teacher when instruction is individualized.

Perhaps the most popular type of individualized instruction is programmed learning in which students have their own materials and work independently. In most programs, students move through the same material in exactly the same sequence in order to master certain knowledge or skills. Individual differences are allowed for by letting students proceed at their own rate. Variations permit students to work through the objectives in different orders or to skip some objectives when it is deemed feasible and desirable. The assumption is made that students will work on self-contained materials and will need little or no assistance from the teacher. In actuality, students will still need assistance, reassurance, attention, approval, and interaction from the teacher and from other students no matter how self-contained the materials are reputed to be. The teacher has to be the student's major resource in such a situation; to ask another student for help will interfere with the latter's progress through the program. Students who are very goal-directed will finish their programs and continually ask the teacher for additional work, while students who are less excited about working alone will seek teacher attention just to have someone to talk to. It takes a great deal of teacher time and effort to construct an individualized classroom, and a great deal of attention and assistance will have to be given to each student on a one-to-one basis.

MYTH 3: *Less teacher time is needed when programmed, individualized materials are used.*

Closely related to Myth 2 is the myth that individualizing instruction will save teacher time. A great deal of teacher time is required to plan the units, give students help as they progress through the materials, diagnose student abilities and learning styles, evaluate student learning, and serve as the major resource for the students. Much more sophisticated teacher skills are needed in diagnosis and evaluation and in individual consulting and counseling. Since the teacher is the major resource for each student, much more teacher time and emotional commitment is demanded.

MYTH 4: *Individualizing instruction will increase the effectiveness of schooling.*

Switching from a competitive to an individualistic classroom will *not* significantly improve the quality of education. There is no evidence that an individualized approach will improve student accomplishment of cognitive and affective outcomes desired by educators. The research evidence indicates that achievement in cognitive areas will not be superior to achievement in competitive goal structures (and will be inferior to achievement in cooperative goal structures) and that the accomplishment of affective outcomes will be seriously lacking. Thus, individualizing instruction will *not* increase the effectiveness of schooling.

MYTH 5: *All students will experience success in an individualized classroom.*

In a competitive classroom, most students will experience failure. Advocates of individualized instruction have made claims that success will be enjoyed by all when a teacher individualizes. The argument goes that if all students can proceed through a set of programmed materials and get answers to questions on the material correctly, they will all experience success. Yet when success is defined as a positive emotional experience, it is clear that answering a question correctly does not necessarily result in positive feelings. Experiencing success will depend upon the student's commitment to the learning goals, the student's freedom to work toward goal accomplishment in the way he thinks best, a goal offering a challenge in which there is a moderate risk of failure, and a goal having relevance to the student's life (Johnson, 1970). Much of the programmed learning material preselected and organized by the curriculum writer turns out to be a situation which is constructed so that the material is not challenging and where the student is not free to choose his own goals or his own procedures for goal accomplishment. Thus while a student may go through a program marking the correct answers, she will most likely be experiencing psychological failure rather than psychological success.

MYTH 6: *Individualized instruction is the only alternative to traditional interpersonal competition.*

In the past, teachers have often believed that the only alternative to competition was individualizing. Anyone who has read this far, however, knows that cooperation is also an alternative.

MYTH 7: *Individualizing instruction will improve classroom climate and learning processes.*

Some advocates of individualized instruction insist that relationships among students and between the teacher and the students will be improved when this goal structure is used. In actuality, when students work under an individualistic goal structure, the social development of the student will suffer, as little interaction will take place among students. Interpersonal and group skills will not be learned and utilized, student friendships and support systems will be minimized, and student loneliness and alienation will result. All the affective outcomes resulting from interaction with other students will be lost. Thus the process of learning will create new undesirable outcomes and consequences, which may increase student dislike for schooling and student dissatisfaction with instruction!

MYTH 8: *Individualizing instruction will facilitate student development of a strong personal identity.*

Rugged individualists often believe that personal identity is built through facing the world alone and achieving without any assistance or help from others. Nothing could be further from the truth. A person's identity is formed by his differentiating himself from others. As the theories of the development of self-identity all state (see Johnson, 1970, 1974c), cooperative interaction, in which a person learns to view himself as others view him, is absolutely necessary. Lack of interaction with other students may seriously interfere with a well-formulated awareness of one's capabilities, uniqueness, and identity.

"Be thou thine own home, and in thyself dwell."   John Donne

"The man who goes alone can start today, but he who travels with another must wait till that other is ready."   Henry David Thoreau

"If everybody minded their own business, "said the Duchess in a hoarse growl," The world would go round a deal faster than it does."
Lewis Carroll

"God helps them that help themselves."   Benjamin Franklin

"If a man does not keep pace with his companions, perhaps it is because he hears a different drummer. Let him step to the music he hears however measured or far away."   Henry David Thoreau

"How many a thing which we cast to the ground, when others pick it up becomes a gem!"
George Meredith

"Raphael paints wisdom, Handel sings it, Phidias carves it, Shakespeare writes it, Wren builds it, Columbus sails it, Luther preaches it, Washington arms it, Watt mechanizes it."   Ralph Waldo Emerson

MYTHS ABOUT COOPERATIVE GOAL STRUCTURES

There are myths about cooperation that have discouraged some teachers from trying it. Frequently, when one of the authors starts to tell a group of teachers about the benefits of cooperative goal structures, a series of questions are asked that reflect myths concerning cooperation perpetuated by the use of competitive and individualistic goal structures. This chapter would not be complete if these myths were not discussed.

MYTH 1: When cooperation is used, all students must work together, and the student who wants to work by himself for a while is forbidden to do so.

The fear of the possible tyranny of groups is the source of several myths about cooperation. Yet it is clear that in a cooperative goal structure a division of labor is always possible in which different students work on different subtasks. Such a division of labor allows students to work by themselves much of the time and join the group only to synthesize everyone's contributions. Cooperation is based upon the mutuality of goals, not upon working in a group.

MYTH 2: Cooperation among students will enslave the gifted while giving the stupid a "free lunch."

As we have pointed out several times in this book, there are advantages to having cooperative groups that are heterogeneous in terms of student abilities. There is a myth that such practices will reduce the achievement of gifted students. Yet there is considerable evidence that the achievement of bright students increases when they participate in heterogeneous groups (Johnson, 1970; Wodarski et al. 1973). In addition, they develop social skills and democratic values that are beneficial to society as well as to each individual.

MYTH 3: Students who do not contribute to the group's work or who in some way reduce the group's performance will be punished or brutalized.

The authors have heard teachers speculating that students would be physically beat up if they could not do as well on a task as the other group members. This belief is a myth because the processes of cooperation—effective communication, mutual liking, helping and sharing, valuing of differences, and so on—will all work in the opposite direction from punishment and rejection. Within a cooperative goal structure students recognize that everyone has different abilities and that the student who is poor in one area may be quite valuable to the group in another area. The potential for a division of labor, furthermore, makes it possible to utilize everyone's varying talents without requiring every student to do the same thing. There is evidence that low achieving students are *not* disliked in a cooperative group (Wodarski et al. 1973).

MYTH 4: Many students will (through apathy) do no work, learn nothing, and yet receive the benefits of the work of other students.

This belief leaves out the increased commitment and pleasure that cooperative structures promote for instructional tasks. Within the traditional competitive goal structure, many students become apathetic and refuse to work, not because they are lazy but because of the nature of a competitive situation in which most students "lose" most of the time. Within a cooperative goal structure, the opportunity for every student to experience psychological success and receive support from his peers will minimize the possibility of student apathy.

MYTH 5: Cooperative goal structures will result in students doing the things they are good at and never working on skills and knowledge that are difficult for them.

This viewpoint ignores the intrinsic motivation upon which performance in cooperative situations is based. There is a great deal of satisfaction to be gained in extending your competence and learning new information and skills when there is a supportive and helpful learning climate. It is within the competitive goal structure that failure is so anxiety-provoking that students refuse to take risks in developing new skills and information.

MYTH 6: If students work together cooperatively they will lose their personal identities because the group will force them to conform to its standards.

Nothing could be further from the truth. You establish your personal identity through cooperative interaction with others, by noting your uniqueness and differentiating yourself from others. Cooperative interaction is an absolute necessity for the establishment of a personal identity. For a full discussion of the development of self-identity, see Johnson (1970).

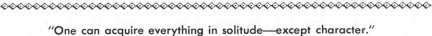

"One can acquire everything in solitude—except character."

Henri Beyle

"No man is an island, entire of itself; every man is a piece of the continent, a part of the main."

John Donne

"Not vain the weakest, if their force unite."

Homer

"United we stand, divided we fall."

Aesop

"Union gives strength."

Aesop

"Two heads are better than one."

Heywood

"All for one, one for all, that is our device."

Dumas

"The true security is to be found in social solidarity rather than in isolated individual effort."

Dostoyevsky

"If we would seek for one word that describes society better than any other, the word is cooperation."

Montagu

". . . There is no violent struggle between plants, no warlike mutual killing, but a harmonious development on a share-and-share-alike basis. The cooperative principle is stronger than the competitive one."   Frits W. Went, *Plants*

CONCLUDING COMMENT

Most of the reasons for using competitive goal structures are more myth than reality. The belief that individualizing instruction is the only alternative or the best alternative to competition is also a myth. Many of the fears some teachers have about the use of cooperative goal structures are also myths. At this time the vast majority of the research indicates that the cooperative goal structure should be the most frequently used goal structure in the classroom. Yet there are benefits in using competitive and individualistic goal structures occasionally. In the next chapter we shall explore the circumstances under which each of the goal structures should be used.

FOUR

selecting the appropriate
goal structure
no need to flip a coin

In Chapter 1, we defined what goal structures are. In Chapter 2, we discussed the results of the research in terms of the processes of interaction and cognitive and affective outcomes that each of the three goal structures promotes. In Chapter 3, we explored some of the undesirable outcomes of competition and the myths that support the inappropriate use of competitive and individualized goal structures and that prevent the use of cooperation. Given this background, it is now important to look at the conditions under which each of the three goal structures should be used and to consider how a teacher makes a decision to structure a unit of instruction cooperatively, competitively, or individualistically.

The appropriate use of all three goal structures will improve your teaching effectiveness and make your life as a teacher considerably more satisfying and enjoyable. It is the inappropriate use of a goal structure that causes problems for students (and, subsequently, the teacher). But when do you want to use each type of goal structure? When is each type of goal structure desirable? You may have been speculating about these questions as you read the past three chapters. It is now time to clarify this issue.

59

The authors believe that cooperative, competitive, and individualistic goal structures are all effective under certain conditions and that a teacher should use all three depending upon the specific instructional objectives and purposes. Students should be taught the basic skills necessary to function in the three types of goal structures. Each time you plan an instructional session, you should make a decision as to which goal structure will promote the needed classroom climate and interpersonal processes to facilitate the accomplishment of the desired cognitive and affective outcomes.

WHEN IS INTERPERSONAL COMPETITION DESIRABLE?

Despite the potentially destructive effects of competition, there are conditions under which it may be used profitably by teachers. First, competition is effective in increasing student performance on a simple drill activity or a speed-related task when sheer quantity of work is desired on a project that requires little or no help from another person; spelling, vocabulary, math drills, writing practice, word recognition, recall of facts and dates, hand–eye coordination, and athletic contests are examples of such tasks. When the instructional goals are to review, drill, or achieve quantity on a simple task, the teacher will wish to use competition. Second, when competition takes place during low-anxiety-producing, relatively unimportant activities, it often is a source of fun, excitement, and a release of energy. People commonly seek out competition under low-anxiety-producing conditions and enjoy it immensely. Games like Monopoly, poker, checkers, and bridge, sports like tennis, golf, and bowling, and such activities as movie- and playgoing and reading provide competitive experiences either directly or vicariously. Physical competition in which students have a chance to be boisterous are involving, exciting, and fun, even for spectators. When winning or losing does not create a great deal of anxiety for any of the participants, there seems to be a sense of pleasure in matching one's skills and abilities against those of one's peers. When the task is not a life and death matter, one should expect to enjoy the interaction—win or lose.

Third, when there are no set criteria by which students can evaluate their skills and abilities there may be a self-evaluatory drive toward comparing oneself with others to obtain an accurate appraisal of oneself (Festinger, 1950, 1954; Pettigrew, 1967). Sometimes students may wish to compete in order to appraise their skills, make comparative judgments, and learn what they are really capable of doing. But if comparisons are going to be made, it is important for each student to keep track of how the competition is going. The fourth condition, therefore, is that each student is able to monitor the progress of his competitors. Fifth, students will be motivated by the competitive goal structure when they believe that they have a reasonable chance of winning.* Sixth, there must be clear criteria concerning what is a right or a wrong answer. Finally, competition will run smoothly when clear procedures of arbitrating arguments and determining winners is set up and communicated to the students.

◇◆◇

In a large city high school, a teacher had just finished chatting with two students and moved to the front of the class, the signal that class was about to begin. "You've spent the last few weeks doing projects that relate to the 15th, 16th, and 17th centuries," she began, "Now, we'll give you a chance to see what you know about some of the people you've met in your reading." She explained that they were going to play a game called Contemporaries in which one student would name a famous person and describe that person's contribution to his times; the next student would then name a contemporary person and the contribution, and so on. If any student was stuck without a name to contribute, or suggested a name that was challenged and found not to be contemporary, he would drop out until a new game was started. Meanwhile, the game would continue until one student was the winner.

The teacher divided the class into groups of five using a list that grouped students in such a way that each student in a cluster had a reasonable chance to win. The students jumped into the game with great enthusiasm and obvious enjoyment. Occasionally, there was a burst of laughter when a name came up that was obviously not contemporary, or when a challenged student was proven correct and the challenger had to drop out. Near the end of the period, the teacher stopped the game and gave the winners from each group a chance to try their skill against each other, establishing temporarily a class champion. The last few minutes before the bell were spent discussing the several instances

---

* The two authors once decided that they had a reasonable chance to win a foot race with their dad. At the time the two authors were four and five years old, and their father was twenty-seven. We decided that an old man of twenty-seven would not be very much competition! So we refused to come home for dinner, thinking he could never catch us. A short race and some swiftly administered physical aversive stimuli ended all motivation to race our father again in the future.

Appropriate Conditions Chart

	Cooperative	Individualized	Competitive
Type of Instructional Activity	Problem solving; divergent thinking or creative tasks; assignments can be more ambiguous with students doing the clarifying, decision making, and inquiring.	Specific skill or knowledge acquisition; assignment is clear and behavior specified to avoid confusion and need for extra help.	Skill practice; knowledge recall and review; assignment is clear with rules for competing specified.
Perception of Goal Importance	Goal is perceived as important for each student, and students expect group to achieve the goal.	Goal is perceived as important for each student, and each student expects eventually to achieve his goal.	Goal is *not* perceived to be of large importance to the students, and they can accept either winning or losing.
Student Expectations	Each student expects positive interaction with other students; sharing of ideas and materials; support for risk taking; making contributions to the group effort; dividing the task among group members; to capitalize on diversity among group members.	Each student expects to be left alone by other students; to take a major part of the responsibility for completing the task; to take a major part in evaluating his progress toward task completion and the quality of his effort.	Each student expects to have an equal chance of winning; to enjoy the activity (win or lose); to monitor the progress of his competitors; to compare ability, skills, or knowledge with peers'.
Expected Source of Support	Other students are perceived to be the major resource for assistance, support, and reinforcement.	Teacher is perceived to be the major resource for assistance, support, and reinforcement.	Teacher is perceived to be the major resource for assistance, support, and reinforcement.

where many in the class didn't realize that two famous people were contemporaries; and what it would take to be able to win next time. After class, the teacher jotted down a few notes about things she had noticed or overheard, observing especially where students seemed to have difficulty with the competition.

How appropriate is this instance of competition? Check it out with the criteria summarized above.

◇◇◇

WHEN IS INTERGROUP COMPETITION DESIRABLE?

The conditions under which a teacher may wish to use intergroup competition may be more common than the conditions under which a teacher may wish to use interpersonal competition. Everything stated above about interpersonal competition applies to intergroup competition also. But there is evidence that association with a group cushions the normal effects of failure (Myers, 1962; Fiedler, 1967); when a group loses, the loss may be taken less personally by each of the group's members. Much of the research comparing cooperation with competition actually compared interpersonal competition with intragroup cooperation–intergroup competition. Thus many of the benefits of cooperation may be obtained when groups compete. Some aspects of intergroup competition may enable a teacher to increase control over the classroom behavior of students and increase the influence of academic norms on students' behavior. Intergroup competition may promote peer group pressure for academic achievement. When there is a great deal of conflict and hostility among class members, placing enemies in a cooperative group that engages in competition with other groups may do much to resolve the conflict (Sherif, 1966; Johnson and Lewicki, 1969).

When even small failures may damage student self-attitudes, when teachers want to promote both cooperation and competition simultaneously, to encourage peer group pressure for academic achievement, and to reduce interpersonal hostility, they may wish to use intergroup competition for instructional purposes.

WHEN IS INDIVIDUALIZED INSTRUCTION DESIRABLE?

Available research comparing student performance in cooperative and individualized situations indicates that cooperation is usually preferable. The authors, however, think that there are conditions under which an individualized approach should be used. When there is a specific skill (such as using a microscope or a calculator) or a specific series of facts (such as important dates in American history) to be learned, when there are enough materials and adequate space so that students can comfortably work on their own, and if programmed materials or other clear procedures are available for such learning, the teacher may wish to individualize the instruction. In such a case the instructional goal is perceived as important for each student to achieve, and each student is perceived as being able to achieve the goal. Students will expect to be left alone by other students in order to complete the program, to take responsibility for completing the program, and to evaluate their own progress. In an individualized situation the teacher becomes the major resource for assistance, and a great deal of teacher time may be needed to monitor and assist the students. If the teacher, in addition, has to write out individualized units, the use of individualized instruction becomes an impossible task.

◇◇

In a ninth grade English class, the students have been reading a cluster of novels centering on the building of the railroad in the western United States. The teacher has done some work with the class on character analysis, i.e., finding out about the appearance, personality, and point of view of major characters in the stories. He now explains to the class that he has the names of several people from the novels in the box he is holding, and in a moment each student will draw a name. Their assignment is to spend the next few days finding out as much as they can about their characters by reading appropriate passages in the novels and by using any other resources they can find. At the end of the week, there will be a number of debates on questions about the building of the railroad, and each student will be expected to introduce himself and argue the point of view of the character he drew from the box. Until the debate each student is to work on his own, gathering the necessary information on his person; if he needs help, he is to come to the teacher so as not to intrude on the work of the other students. The students eagerly await their chance to draw a name and begin their research. The teacher will work with each student through the next few days to see that each has all the materials needed and has mastered the perspective of the character he or she has drawn, so that all can each contribute to the debates on Friday.

Does this instance of the Individualistic goal structure seem appropriate? Check with the criteria listed above.

◇◇

Now there's a way to teach
each student in the class
as if he were the only student
in the class.

Reprinted by permission of PLAN * Individualized Learning System Division, Westinghouse Learning Corporation.

WHEN IS COOPERATION DESIRABLE?

Beyond all doubt, cooperation should be the most frequently used goal structure. The conditions under which it is effective and desirable are almost too many to list. Whenever problem solving is desired, whenever divergent thinking or creativity is desired, whenever quality of performance is expected, whenever the task is complex, when the learning goals are highly important, and when the social development of students is one of the major instructional goals, cooperation should be used. Students will expect the group to achieve the learning goal, and they will also expect to have positive interaction with other students, to share ideas and materials, to get group support for taking risks in thinking and trying out skills, to have every member contribute in some way to goal achievement, and to divide the task between each other in a division of labor when desirable. When a teacher wishes to promote positive interaction among students, a facilitative learning climate, a wide range of cognitive and affective outcomes, and positive relations between himself and the students, cooperative goal structures will be used. In a cooperative situation the students will perceive the other students as the major resource and source of support, freeing the teacher to manage the total classroom situation. Cooperation needs to be used to promote the long-term socialization goals of education and to train students in interpersonal skills and the capability to assume membership in stable relationships and families. Since cooperation has been discussed extensively in the previous chapters, all the conditions under which it should be used will not be detailed here.

DECIDING ON A GOAL STRUCTURE

How do you decide which goal structure to use? What are the steps in planning you will have to go through in order to make a decision? You will put yourself on the appropriate track in structuring your teaching if you answer the following questions:

1. What do I want the students to obtain from this instructional experience? What cognitive and affective outcomes do I want them to achieve?
2. What is the nature of the instructional task? Is it problem solving, skill practice, or mastery of facts?
3. What type of instructional climate and interaction among students is necessary to facilitate the accomplishment of the learning objecives?

4. How simple or complex are the instructional tasks? Do students need a great deal of assistance and resources? If yes, who would be the most appropriate resource, other students or the teacher?

5. Is the instructional task new or review-application?

6. What learning outcomes does each goal structure tend to promote? (Review Chapter 2.)

7. What processes of interaction and climate does each goal structure tend to promote? (Review Chapter 2.)

8. Under what conditions should each goal structure be used? (Review the previous sections of this chapter.)

9. Which structure is the most appropriate for this instructional session?

Matching the goal structure and the learning activity is the most important step in structuring your classroom. It needs to be done carefully, especially at first. When instruction is not going well, the first question to ask is whether the goal structure is appropriate. "Am I using the appropriate goal structure?" will be a standard question for you.

FREQUENCY OF USE OF EACH GOAL STRUCTURE

As a teacher, you will use all three goal structures over a period of time. What types of learning goals and what type of classroom climate you prefer will determine the frequency with which you use each one. Most teachers spend a large proportion of their time in promoting problem-solving skills that give maximum thinking experience to the students, tasks that are best served by a cooperative goal structure. To a lesser extent, there are important and specific skills and knowledge that can best be mastered by studying under an individualistic goal structure. Tasks calling for drill or review of facts are best suited to a competitive goal structure and probably require the least amount of time in most classes. Thus a cooperative goal structure may be used 70 percent of the time, individualistic 20 percent of the time, and competitive 10 percent of the time. With students perceiving school as predominantly competitive, and with cooperation being used systematically in very few classrooms, your task in training students to shift quickly from one goal structure to another and to function primarily within a cooperative goal structure will not at first be an easy one. The following chapters will explain how to implement and monitor each goal structure, how to evaluate students within each goal structure, and what skills students need to learn in order to behave appropriately in all three types of situations.

COMBINING GOAL STRUCTURES

Throughout this book we discuss each goal structure separately. Yet any experienced teacher knows that various combinations are used. Probably the most frequent combination will be cooperative and individualized programs. While working on a cooperative task, a group may arrive at a division of labor in which it is necessary for different students to master different skills or different information in order to provide the resources the group needs to achieve its goal successfully. In such cases, individual learning programs may be the most efficient approach. Then the group members will meet and integrate their resources in order to provide the group with a problem solution of high quality. The advantages to such a procedure are that information is best comprehended and applied when discussed in a cooperative group, and that the learning of all is increased when members of a discussion group have different information and points of view. An ideal teaching situation is to assign a cooperative project and provide individualized programs for various aspects of the problem so that different group members can master different skills and information for later integration into the group's product.

◇◇

As you walk into the classroom, you see that the students are spread out so that each has as much individual space as possible. Each student has a kit of materials (in this case, a pencil, scissors, and several measuring devices). The teacher has just completed handing out instructions to each student. He describes to the class as a whole how to get started on the instructions. A few minutes go by, and hands start appearing in the air and students look puzzled. The teacher begins to move around the room, answering each student's questions. He pauses, wondering what is the matter; the instructions were supposed to explain everything, and he thought they were very clear. As more hands appear, the teacher is not able to respond to all the students seeking help, and some muttering is heard. "Don't bother the other students," the teacher says. "I'll get to you as soon as I can!" Yet the students begin to talk with each other, trying to figure out what to do.

Why is this teacher having a problem? What could you do to salvage the lesson?

The teacher stops and thinks to himself. "What am I going to do now? Obviously, the task isn't easy to them, and I can't get around to everyone. Perhaps if students work together they can figure out what to do." The teacher divides the students into groups of three and, after explaining the instructions to the class as a whole, asks the students to work together to complete the assignment. The waving hands disappear, and an industrious murmur settles over the classroom as the students begin to solve the problems detailed in the instructions.

The teacher in this classroom was using an inappropriate goal structure and, fortunately, was able to switch. Changing the goal structure won't always solve a teacher's problem, but it is a good place to look first.

◇◇

teachers are bridge builders who put theory into practice

FIVE

implementing goal structures
building a bridge
from theory to practice

This chapter is designed to assist you in setting up the different goal structures and to implement them. The major things you need to consider are pointed out, and the procedures are described.

What does your mental picture of each goal structure look like? The series of photographs on pages 74–76 represent cooperative, individualized, and competitive instructional situations. How do the photographs compare with your mental images? If you were to take these pictures in your classroom, how would they be different?

We are hoping this book will help real teachers in real classrooms teaching real students, so we attempt to be specific in our suggestions. You must realize, however, that following a "recipe" never gives the best results. We have seen many teachers who never got beyond the initial "recipe" stage of development in teaching a unit or a curriculum. We have been tempted to follow recipes ourselves at times when we did not have a clear, internalized idea of what should be done. In implementing appropriate goal structures, you will have to consider such factors as your own teaching style, your students, your instructional objectives, and the general learning situation. Although at first you may follow our suggestions point for point, you should expect to evolve and find your own ways to implement the goal structures in your particular situation. The monitoring of student behavior and the evaluation of student performance will be discussed in later chapters. Your responsibilities and the procedures for arranging your room, communicating the goal structures to students, communicating your expectations for student behavior within each goal structure, assigning students to groupings of appropriate size, and using mixtures of goal structures will all be discussed in this chapter. Within these activities you will find a variety of implications for your instructional role as a teacher. Perhaps the most important implication is that goal structuring will allow the focus to be on the learner, not on the teacher. The student will be doing the thinking and the behaving while you assist, monitor, and share in the learning experience. It is important for you to remember that you are not responsible for student learning; only the student can make himself learn. You are responsible for structuring the situation so that student learning is facilitated and so that students who wish to learn have an optimal opportunity for doing so.

It is entirely possible that you are already using many of the suggested procedures included in this chapter. In that case, the chapter may help you to be more consistent in developing a particular goal structure or may give you other ideas about how you may support your present procedures. Keep your present practices rolling.

◇◇◇

IT WON'T BE EASY FOR YOU OR THE STUDENTS

TO MOVE TO

THE IDEALLY STRUCTURED CLASSROOM.

EXPECT TO EVOLVE.

◇◇◇

MAKE THE MOST OF IT!

The format of this chapter requires dialogue between you and us, and perhaps between you and others interested in classroom goal structures. We want you to react to and speculate about the things that are said and to use your background in solving the problem of how and when to set up a certain goal structure. It is for this reason that we ask a lot of questions and occasionally are impolite enough to suggest that you should get out a piece of paper, study a photograph, or reflect on an anecdote. Some suggestions to make the procedures described in this chapter more useful are:

1. Consider the questions as pre-cuing the material following them. Pause a moment and reflect before continuing your reading. The questions also make good openers for discussing the material with others.
2. Feel free to mark up the chapter, and the book, by underlining things you see as important; write notes and questions in the margins to keep track of disagreements or procedural reminders relating to your own situation. (Please consult the owner of the book before you begin marking it up.)
3. Have a particular classroom in mind as you read the chapter (your own or one that you are observing). Having a "reality referent" will help you react to the material being presented.
4. Have some friends, fellow students, fellow teachers, or a spouse available to discuss the ideas and suggestions. Examining your present classroom goal structures and planning how to implement a new goal structure in your classroom are problem-solving situations where a cooperative goal structure is appropriate. Being a member of a cooperating group is the most reasonable way to approach this book.

◇◇◇

PLEASE TAKE THE TIME

TO MAKE THE PROCEDURES DISCUSSED

YOURS, NOT OURS!

◇◇◇

Let's take a look at your present classroom goal structure(s). One way is to do a mental survey by closing your eyes and walking through an instructional week. How does Monday morning start (besides sleepily)? We have talked to many teachers who have no idea how Mondays begin and who only vaguely remember any part of Monday. If that is your case, start with Tuesday morning. What is the first instructional block of time? Which goal structure dominates? Move on systematically through the day; move on systematically through the week. On the basis of the preceding chapters, where are your goal structures inappropriate? Why? Take notes on your mental survey and then discuss them with two other persons who are also taking a mental survey of their instructional week.

Next, review how heavily you depend on each goal structure in a given day or week. The authors believe that teachers should use cooperative goal

LEARNING
RESOURCES
CENTER

LANGUAGE LAB

2ND FLOOR

MON-THURS 8-10
FRIDAY 8-6
SATURDAY 9-6
SUNDAY . . . . . . closed

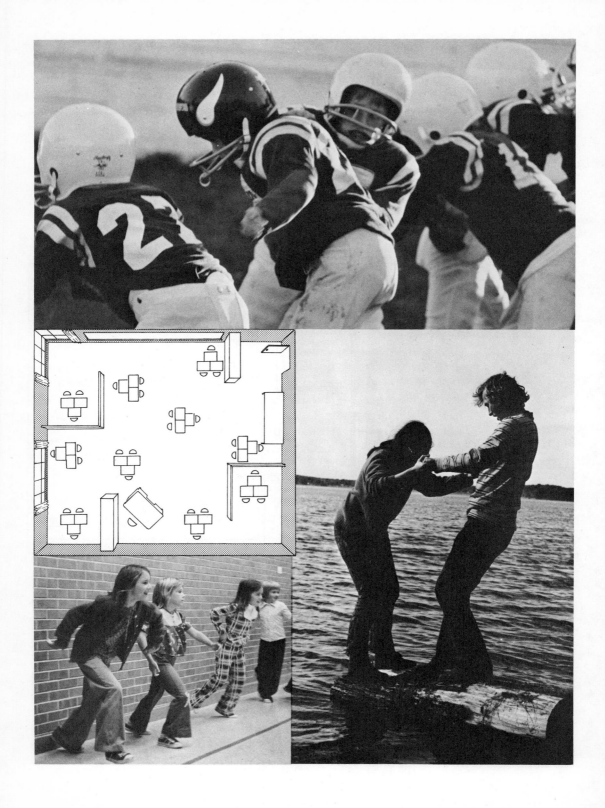

structures the most, individualistic goal structures next, and competitive goal structures least. Remember that implementing a goal structure does not mean that students will automatically behave appropriately; they must correctly perceive the goal structure, understand what is expected from them, and have the prerequisite skills.

IMPLEMENTING A GOAL STRUCTURE

Now to the difficult part: how do you implement an appropriate goal structure for your desired instructional outcomes? You have probably already developed a mental picture of what each goal structure will look like when it is operating in your classroom. In developing this mental image further, consider the following questions:

1. What are the desired cognitive and affective outcomes for the lesson you are imagining?
2. How does the physical organization of the classroom relate to the goal structure being used? Does the room arrangement facilitate the needed student access to other students, the teacher, and the needed materials?
3. What is the nature and amount of interaction among students, between the students and the teacher, and between the students and the instructional materials and equipment?
4. What are your responsibilities as a teacher in the situation?
5. How can you tell whether student behavior is appropriate to the goal structure?
6. How will you evaluate student performance?
7. How much are you enjoying the teacher role in the instructional situation?

CLASSROOM ARRANGEMENT

How do you arrange the classroom to facilitate each goal structure? Could you walk into a classroom and tell by its arrangement whether it was set up for a cooperative, individualistic, or competitive goal structure? Perhaps glancing at the photographs again will give you further ideas. At this point, take out a piece of paper and draw three diagrams to show how you would arrange your own classroom to facilitate each type of goal structure. How do your arrangements compare (or improve upon) our photographs? Which goal structure do you tend to use most frequently? How can you shift from one goal structure to another with the least amount of time and trouble?

If you need more space than is available in your classroom, what "spill-over" space is available for your use in the rest of the building?

There are distinct classroom arrangements for the appropriate use of each goal structure. Each arrangement has to take into account the necessary student access to other students, to the teacher, and to the instructional materials. In a cooperative learning situation the classroom has to be organized so that students are clustered together in groups (so they can focus on each other and on shared materials and equipment), with clear access lanes to each other, to other groups, and to materials. The teacher must have clear access to the groups in order to observe and consult with them during the lesson. In an individualized learning situation the classroom has to be organized so that students are isolated from each other, seated at separate desks or carrels spaced as far apart as possible, do not have clear access lanes to each other or to general materials (each student needs to have his own self-contained set of materials), but do have clear access lanes to the teacher. In a competitive learning situation the classroom has to be organized so that students' desks are arranged in clusters (so they can keep track of each other's progress for comparison purposes—"Am I ahead or behind the other students?"), do not have clear access lanes to general materials or to other clusters, but do have a clear access lane to the teacher. In all three types of learning situations the teacher needs to be able to move from student to student or from cluster to cluster in order to provide help and assistance or to observe what is taking place.

Especially in the cooperative goal structure, students' seats should be arranged so that each student can see all the other members of his group and can be heard without needing to shout (and disturb the other groups). Small groups may work at a table, sitting as close to one another as is comfortable, push desks together, or sit in a tight circle. These small groups should be spaced in the classroom in such a way as to maximize the distance between them. Larger groups can be formed into a double semi-circle or horseshoe of chairs.

Since the individualistic goal structure needs some isolation where students can pursue their goals independently, the library or study centers can be valuable annexes to the classroom. Some form of study carrels are useful when students need to work independently.

GOAL STRUCTURING

Consider the definition of each goal structure presented in Chapter 1 and what the definitions suggest in terms of how instructional tasks are to be completed. *How do you establish a goal structure so that the appropriate method of task accomplishment is likely to result?* Consider the following situation.

You have just presented a problem to a group of students by asking how long a candle will burn in a quart jar. Instead of a single answer, the class comes up with a range of answers that are the results of their experiments. You ask why all students didn't get the same answer, and the students suggest that the shape of the quart jar and whether or not a previous candle has been burned in the jar may affect the answers. You then ask, "How many things can our group find that make a difference in how long the candle burns?" A large piece of paper is taped to the wall to collect suggestions, and the students are encouraged to check out their ideas with each other and have other students double check suggestions by repeating the experiment.

The goal structure suggested in this situation is cooperative. The important things to remember in setting up a cooperative goal structure are:

1. *Present the goal as a group goal.* In this situation, the search for variables is directed at the group rather than at each individual, and the shared list will belong to the group, not to an individual member.

2. *Facilitate and encourage the sharing of ideas and materials.* The group list is one way of doing this. Determining whether the shape of the jar is an important variable will involve sharing of results or exchanging different-shaped jars within the group. Students should be encouraged to help each other with the experiment and in formulating conclusions.

3. *Facilitate and encourage a division of labor where appropriate.* It would be appropriate to have all the students involved in brainstorming possible variables at the beginning of the instructional session, but a division of labor may result in which some students think up possible variables and other students conduct the experiments necessary to check the ideas out. Another division of labor would be subgroups of students checking out different variables for the group.

4. *Reward the group for successful completion of the task.* Since the list of variables affecting the time a candle burns is a group product, all students share in the successful development of the list. Emphasize that the group has successfully completed the instructional task. Direct most feedback to the group and avoid praising only a few of the group members. Since all members will benefit from each other's work and since different members will make different contributions to the group's success, every individual member will experience success when the group successfully completes the instructional task. In order to evaluate the quality of the group product, you will need a set of criteria indicating different levels of adequacy. Each group should be aware of these criteria as they work on the task. It is important to avoid comparisons among students as to the quality of their work, since such comparisons will promote competition and undermine cooperation.

In a cooperative goal structure, students work together to produce one product. If students are each producing a product that they do not integrate into one, the goal structure is not cooperative.

Consider the following situation:

You have just handed out a four-page programmed booklet on how to use a microscope. You explain, "For some of the things we are going to be doing, each student will need to know how to use a microscope. I'll give each of you a microscope and the other things you will need to work through this booklet. Take your time and work carefully until you have mastered the tasks outlined in the booklet. Let me know if you need help with anything." You then see that each student has a microscope and kit of materials and will begin to move from student to student to see how they are progressing.

The goal structure being suggested in this situation is individualistic. It is appropriate because the goal carries the expectation that each student will achieve mastery of some specific information and skill. You need to keep in mind the following things:

1. *Present the goal as one for each student to achieve without regard to the goal accomplishment of other students.* In this situation, the goal is for each student to master the use of the microscope as described by the programmed booklet. Speed is not an issue.

2. *Facilitate and encourage each student to work on his or her own.* The use of the programmed booklet and kit of materials is one method of structuring independence. Stating that students should seek help from the teacher rather than from other students is another way. Students should be discouraged from interrupting each other. It would be appropriate to encourage some students to go beyond the specified program and try out ideas of their own, such as making extra slides to examine through their microscopes.

3. *Reward each student separately on the basis of her or his progress toward the successful completion of the instructional task.* Systematically praise, reward, and encourage each student while monitoring progress on a one-to-one basis. This means that the teacher, not other students, is the person who gives praise for good work.

80

Consider this third situation.

> *After you have spent some time demonstrating how candles burn in jars under different conditions, bring in a few odd-sized and odd-shaped jars. Ask, "Which one of you can give me the best estimate of how long a candle will burn in this jar?" and hold up one of the jars. Arrange the classroom so that students are in small clusters and can see how they are doing in comparison with other students. Do not make the reward for winning so important that students will lose the spirit of fun in the competition. Let the students study the jar and write down their estimates on a slip of paper. Let each student share his estimates with the competitors in the cluster. There is a feeling of excitement as you light the candle and place the jar over it. When the candle goes out, there is good-natured congratulating of the winners.*

The goal structure suggested in this situation is a competitive. That the situation is appropriately structured is evidenced in the enjoyment the students get in competing in a review of something they have already studied and in the fact that all students believe they have a good chance of "winning." The situation is viewed not as a crucial test, but more as an interlude as they continue to learn about the factors involved with burning candles in jars. In setting up a competitive goal structure, keep the following things in mind:

1. *Present the goal of "winning" as doing better than the other students in the cluster.* In this situation, the one who makes the most accurate estimate will "win."
2. *Facilitate and encourage each student to work on her own with a planned way for her to monitor the progress and/or product of the other students in her cluster.* What other students do establishes the criteria for her success or failure in this situation. Each estimate is shared so that the students will know who won.
3. *Reward each student on the basis of how well he does compared to the other students.* Congratulate the winner in each cluster. You may also rank the students from most accurate to least accurate to establish degrees of winning. Make sure the reward for winning is not so important to the students that the good-natured fun of the competition is lost. One of the advantages of having small clusters within which students compete is that there will be several winners within any classroom. If there is a desire to see who the best estimator in the room is, you can compare the estimates of the winners in each cluster.

When assigning a goal structure to students, it is important to let them know what they are expected to accomplish (i.e., group product or individual product and the specific nature of the product) and how long they have to work on it. Otherwise, the ambiguity of the situation produces confusion and hostility, which severely limits the possibility of productive learning activity. In a problem-solving situation, assignments are sometimes designed to be intentionally vague or ambiguous so that students practice decision making and group goal setting. When giving the assignment and setting up a cooperative goal structure, you should explain the reason for this ambiguity; you may also want to give the group a specific time limit on solving the problem. Whichever goal structure you implement, you will want to make very clear what the instructional goal is and how long the students have to accomplish it. For a detailed discussion of setting goals, see Johnson and Johnson (1975).

EXPECTATIONS

Perhaps even more important than the arrangement of the classroom and the setting of goals is the question of how students perceive the use of each other, the teacher, and the materials within the classroom (or instructional area). Teachers need to make their expectations clear in each of these areas. Let us return to the first situation.

> *In searching for the variables that affect the length of time a candle burns in a jar, the students have collected their equipment and are working in clusters of two's or three's, or by themselves, on the problem. The materials, several jars and candles of different sizes and shapes, are centrally located. There is a lot of movement and chatting among the students, and the list of possible variables is growing as students write their ideas on the large sheet of paper taped to the blackboard. The teacher moves around, listening to discussions and watching the experimenting. Occasionally he joins in with a comment or takes time to try an experiment, writing a suggested variable on the class paper.*

In this classroom the teacher has made clear the following expectations:

1. *Students should perceive each other as a major resource.* It is not only okay for students to talk with each other and move around the room to see what others are doing, it is expected.
2. The teacher serves as a catalyst in making suggestions and in supplying *extra equipment suggested by the students, but she is not the primary resource.* The teacher expects the students to call on her less and less as they begin to use each other more and more for ideas and verification of solutions.

3. A *wide variety* of materials is available, rather than a standard set of materials for each student (i.e., a jar, a candle, matches), and sharing of materials is expected. The cooperative structure profits from passing the materials back and forth along with ideas and results.

Now let's return to the second situation.

After seeing that each student has his own kit of materials and a separate place to work, the teacher moves from student to student to oversee individual progress and act as a resource. The students are working with their kits as they read through the instructions, occasionally raising their hands to signal the teacher that they need something. As they concentrate on learning to use the microscopes and making slides, they seem relatively unaware of the other students. As they finish, they report to the teacher and ask what to work on next.

In the individualistic goal structure described here, the teacher let the students know that she expected each one (1) to work alone without paying attention to or interacting with other students, (2) to use the teacher as their major resource, and (3) to have a complete set of materials.

The use of carrels and other separation techniques is common. Since each student is working on his own task at his own pace, student-student interaction is intrusive and not helpful. Students should expect periodic visits from the teacher but should start out with a clear understanding of the assignment so that a minimum of extra explanation is required. Programmed materials, task cards, and demonstrations are among the techniques that can be used to facilitate the task.

Let us return to the third situation.

After the students have shared their estimates of how long a candle will burn in the new jar and have found out who had the closest estimate, they persuade the teacher to let them try another jar. The same feeling of excitement pervades the classroom in this competition. After the jar is tested and the winners congratulated, the students move back to their work concerning the variables that affect the length of time a candle burns. Some of the students request the use of the new jars in their experimenting.

In the competitive goal structure, the teacher needs to make clear to the students that he expects each one to: (1) interact in planned and informal ways to keep track of each other's progress, (2) look less to the teacher for judgment of progress and more to comparison with others' progress, and (3) have a set of materials either individually or in common with a cluster of students, according to the demands of the situation (i.e., a game format would call for a cluster).

Although the students are encouraged to share their progress, they are not expected to share ideas or solutions. In this situation, they found out who had won by checking the estimates written in advance, thus sharing their progress but not helping each other. The teacher becomes the primary resource for questions like, "Why didn't I win?" (or "Why did I win?") and "What do I need to do to be able to win next time?"

Expectations for Each Goal Structure of Teacher and Students

	Cooperation	*Individualistic*	*Competition*
Student access to each other	Use each other as major resource.	Minimal use of each other as resource.	Observing or other means of keeping track of each other. Students working in clusters with some movement and talking between students.
	Free movement and talking between students.	Students working on their own with very little movement or talking between students.	
	Students grouped in variety of ways, heterogeneous groups are best.	Students not grouped.	Students grouped in clusters emphasizing equal chance at winning.
Student access to the teacher	Less use of the teacher for ideas and solutions as they use each other more.	High use of teacher for ideas and feedback.	Less use of teacher for ideas, feedback or solutions as criteria of winning are set by each other's performance.
Teacher statements	"Check with your group."	"Don't bother David while he's working."	"Who has the most so far?"
	"Does anyone around you know?"	"Raise your hand if you need help."	"What do you need to do to win next time?"
	"Add your idea to the others on the board."	"Let me know when you're finished."	
Student access to materials	Centrally located, shared set of materials. Large variety with minimal duplication.	Complete set of materials for each student.	Set of materials for each cluster of students, or individual sets for each student.
	Need knowledge of what is available and of ways to share.	Need complete instructions on use of materials initially.	Need rules on how to take turns with common materials.
Room arrangement	Clusters of chairs or use of tables (probably without ownership feelings toward any particular chair).	Separate desks or carrels with as much space between students as can be provided.	Clusters of desks or tables with separation possibilities (moving desks away from each other).

Take out a sheet of paper and write down how you would implement a cooperative, individualized, and competitive goal structure with your class. Take an actual classroom assignment and review the steps presented above. Then write down what you would say to the class to make the assignment a cooperative experience, an individualized experience, and a competitive experience. After you have done so, try them out to see how well what you have written down works!

You may have to repeat your expectations for a goal structure several times while the students adjust to using appropriate goal structures in different situations. If you are having a great deal of difficulty, you should check (1) whether the goal structure is really the appropriate one, (2) whether the goal structure is clear, (3) whether the students understand their role and the role of the teacher, (4) whether the materials and room arrangement facilitate the goal structure, and (5) whether the students have the prerequisite skills for the goal structure being used. After things get started, it is absolutely necessary that you monitor what is going on and determine whether what is happening is what you want to have happen.

MIXED GOAL STRUCTURING

Mixed goal structures can be structured in a variety of ways if the teacher wishes to do so. One way, for example, to structure a combination of cooperative and individualistic goal structures is to reward student performance on ratios such as the following:

1. Students receive 67 percent credit for every problem they solve correctly and 33 percent of the average of the less successful half of their group.
2. Students receive 33 percent credit for every problem they solve correctly and 67 percent credit for the average of the less successful half of their group.

The use of such ratios will not be as effective as pure cooperation in promoting positive student interaction and cognitive and affective outcomes, but it will encourage peer tutoring and helping. With some groups of students, combination ratios may be more effective, although the authors have never seen such a group. As a teacher, however, you should feel free to experiment with a variety of mixtures until you are convinced that you are using the most effective goal structures for your students.

STRUCTURING INTERGROUP COMPETITION

Some teachers prefer the use of intergroup competition in their classrooms. How do they structure such a situation? First, groups are formed within the classroom that are heterogeneous in terms of ability and equally matched across groups. This can be done either through random assignment to groups or by ranking the students in terms of achievement and then randomly assigning students to groups so that each group has an equal number of high, middle, and low pretest students. Six members is a good size for competing groups. Second, the classroom groups compete with each other for rewards given to the highest achieving and best behaved group. Third, since the outcomes of a group depend upon the group average (or the average of the lower half of the group) the entire group benefits or suffers as a consequence of the conduct of individual members. This encourages tutoring and helping among the students. The teacher may wish to review the skills and procedures needed for tutoring within each group with the students and to highlight the importance of cooperation within the group. Fourth, it is important for the teacher to ensure that the intergroup competition does not become so strong that it outweighs the intragroup cooperation. Once competition becomes too serious, all the destructive outcomes of competition will appear, and students resort to bickering, scapegoating, and negative interpersonal relationships. As the saying goes, "It's not whether you win or lose, it's how you play the game." The corollary in this situation would be, "It's not how fiercely you compete with the other groups, it's how comfortably you cooperate with your teammates." What you are losing when you use intergroup competition is the flow of ideas and materials between groups and the overall class possibility of a division of labor. In this combination of cooperation and competition, you need to make clear two sets of expectations: cooperation within the group and competition between the groups.

A group of researchers at Johns Hopkins University led by David DeVries and Keith Edwards have developed a system for using a combination of instructional games and intergroup competition within classrooms. When an instructional game is used for drill activities on material already mastered by the students it facilitates enjoyable competition within the classroom. A class tournament is structured around the game in which *each student competes as a representative of his team* with students of equal aptitude from other teams. Teams are formed so that each team is representative of the entire class with respect to academic ability and various individual characteristics such as sex and ethnic group membership. *Teams are given time to study together* so that peer tutoring can take place, and team membership is held stable for a period of time so that group cohesion and commitment can be built up. In the tournament *team grades are assigned on a competitive basis* so that the teams are ranked from best to worst with the top one or two teams being declared the winners.

A tournament takes place once or twice a week using either published games or teacher-designed games. The procedure for designing your own games for drill purposes is as follows (DeVries, Edwards, and Fennessey, 1973).

General Instructional Game Structure

Materials Needed: (1) Deck of question cards; (2) Rules; (3) Answer sheet

The Rules

1. To start the game, shuffle the deck of cards and place it face down on the table. Decide who will be player number 1. Play is clockwise from player number 1.

2. Each player (when it is his turn) must take the top card from the deck, read it aloud, and do one of two things:
   a. Say he does not know the answer or is not sure of the answer, and ask if another player wants to give an answer. If no one wants to give an answer, the card is placed on the bottom of the deck. If another player gives an answer, he follows the procedure described below.
   b. Answer the question immediately and ask if anyone wants to challenge his answer. The player to the right of the person giving the answer has the first chance to challenge. If he does not wish to challenge, then the player to his right can challenge.

3. If there is no challenge, another player should check the answer. In the lower right-hand corner of each card, there is a letter and a number; use this to find the answer on the answer sheet.
   a. If the answer is correct, the player keeps the card.
   b. If the answer is wrong, the player must place the card on the bottom of the deck.

4. If there is a challenge and the challenger decides not to give an answer:
   a. If the original answer is wrong, the player must place the card on the bottom of the deck.
   b. If the original answer is correct, the player keeps the card and the challenger must give up one of the cards he has already won (if he has any) and place it on the bottom of the deck.

5. If there is a challenge and the challenger gives an answer:
   a. If the challenger's answer is correct, the challenger receives the card.
   b. If the challenger gives the wrong answer, and the original answer is

Sample Game *

Background of the game: The students in a seventh grade English class were studying sentences. In the game they were asked to identify the item as either a complete or an incomplete sentence. If the item was an incomplete sentence, the player had to tell *why* it was incomplete. A sentence was incomplete because either the verb or subject was missing.

We stopped for lunch. (B-4)	A clown and monkey rode at the head of the parade. (B-24)
Leaving the lake in the morning. (B-3)	Leaned out the window. (B-23)

Sentences Game II

Answer Sheet B

B-1	Complete sentence	B-13	Complete sentence
B-2	Complete sentence	B-14	Complete sentence
B-3	Incomplete sentence; no subject	B-15	Incomplete sentence; no subject
B-4	Complete sentence	B-16	Complete sentence
B-5	Incomplete sentence; no verb	B-17	Complete sentence
B-6	Incomplete sentence; no verb	B-18	Incomplete sentence; no verb
B-7	Complete sentence	B-19	Incomplete sentence; no subject
B-8	Complete sentence	B-20	Complete sentence
B-9	Incomplete sentence; no verb	B-21	Incomplete sentence; no verb
B-10	Incomplete sentence; no verb	B-22	Incomplete sentence; no subject
B-11	Incomplete sentence; no verb	B-23	Incomplete sentence; no subject
B-12	Incomplete sentence; no subject	B-24	Complete sentence

◇◇◇

* This game was developed by DeVries, Edwards, and Fennessey in cooperation with Carol Hopkins, a teacher at Northern Parkway Junior High School, Baltimore, Md.

correct, the challenger must give up one of the cards he has already won (if he has any) and place it on the bottom of the deck.

c. If both the challenger's answer and the original answer are wrong, the card is placed on the bottom of the deck.

6. At the end of the game, when there are no more cards in the deck, each player counts up the number of cards he has and records this number as his score. The player who has the most cards is the winner.

The tournament is conducted as follows. First, students are assigned to three-student tournament tables so that each student is placed in competition with two other students, each of whom represents a different group. In order to create equitable competition each table consists of students of comparable academic achievement (as determined by prior performance in the subject area). The assignment of students to tournament tables can be seen in the diagram.

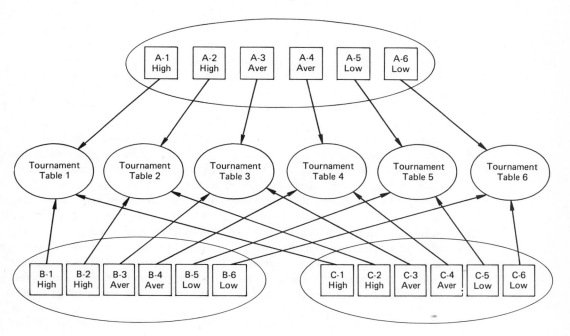

During the tournament the students play the game for 30 to 50 minutes. At the end of a tournament session the students at each table compare their scores to determine the top scorer, the middle scorer, and the low scorer. The game scores are converted into points, with a fixed number of points assigned to the top scorer (6 points), middle scorer (4 points), and the low scorer (2 points) at each table. A team score is obtained by adding the scores of all the individual members. Team scores are then ranked and listed. DeVries and Edwards recommend that a newsletter be used to announce the team standings. The newsletter can be distributed the day following the tournament. Included in the newsletter would be the latest team standings for the grading period, the ranking of the teams on the previous day's tournament, and some commentary about the winners at each table and the performance of the members of the winning team.

WHAT IS THE MOST APPROPRIATE GROUP SIZE?

Whenever you use cooperative or competitive goal structures, you will need to decide on the appropriate group size for the assignment. In an individualized goal structure, students work by themselves, so no decisions concerning group size need to be made. The size of the group in a competitive goal structure can vary from a small cluster to a large group. The thing to keep in mind is that there is only one winner per group and that second place is really not like first place. If you break a class up into several smaller clusters, students will be able to monitor each other's progress more easily, students can be grouped so that each has a reasonable chance of winning and, of course, you will have several winners rather than just one.

What is the optimal size for a cooperative group? The most difficult decisions about the size of groups arise when you use a cooperative goal structure. The optimal size of a group will vary according to the desired processes and outcomes of the assignment, the age of students, the experience students have had in working together, the possibilities for a division of labor, and the number of students in your class. Small groups of six to ten members have been used successfully for cooperative tasks. The group is small enough to allow everyone to take an active part in the discussion, yet large enough to provide the diversity of opinions, information, points of view, and background needed for effective problem solving. Groups larger than ten may have "air time" problems in that all group members may not have enough time to express themselves. When there is limited time available in these larger groups, there may be competition for time to speak or, conversely, students may "opt out." In problem-solving activities, a group size that maximizes each member's participation is preferable, and this may mean using pairs or triads for tasks that require high involvement and are not easily broken down into a division of labor. On the other hand, bringing the whole class together to share ideas and results is sometimes necessary. No rule of thumb is possible in deciding what size group to utilize; the teacher simply has to experiment to determine what size works best for a particular purpose.

One strategy for ensuring total participation and the chance for each student to develop interaction skills is to start the class out in dyads. When they have arrived at an answer, instruct each dyad to join with another dyad and discuss the issue in this group of four until they arrive at an appropriate answer. Proceed to combine groups until the total class is meeting as one group. Although this takes some time to accomplish, the payoff in active participation and involvement may well be worth it, and it gives the teacher a chance to watch students in action in a variety of groups. This exercise may answer some questions you have about optimal group size with your class.

◇◇◇

Setting Up Group Contingencies

There are times when a teacher may wish to reward students using extrinsic reinforcements such as tokens or privileges within the school. When extrinsic reinforcements are used they are made contingent upon certain behaviors and level of performances of students. There are three basic alternative group contingencies that may be used to promote cooperative behavior and achievement. The first is the *average performance group contingency*; all members of a group are reinforced on the basis of the average performance of all of the group members. Alternatively, the group may be reinforced on the basis of the high performances in the group. Thus, the highest scores of one-quarter of the group may be used as a basis for determining reinforcements. This procedure is referred to as a *high performance group contingency*. Finally, a group may be reinforced on the basis of the low performances in the group; the lowest scores of one-quarter of the group are used as a basis for determining reinforcements under a *low performance group contingency*. Research on the use of these three types of group contingencies indicates that the most fruitful is the low performance group contingency. The performance of poor students is greatly raised, both through increased motivation to help their group and through tutoring by the more gifted students. The performance of the more gifted students is not hampered by the use of this group contingency. The overall performance of the group will be highest when the low performance group contingency is used.

◇◇◇

HOW DO YOU ASSIGN STUDENTS TO GROUPS?

There are many ways to form student groups other than by relative ability (believe it or not!). Some form of ability grouping may be appropriate when you form competitive clusters so that each student has a somewhat equal chance of winning, but ability grouping is not suited to cooperation, where heterogeneity pays off. In a cooperative structure, random assignment usually assures a good mixture of boys and girls, highly verbal and passive students, leaders and followers, and enthusiastic and reluctant learners.

◇◇◇

Random assignment can be accomplished by using a count-off procedure, which divides the number of students in the class by the number of members you want in each small group. The result is the highest number to which the students should number-off. For example, if there are twenty-eight students and you want groups of seven students each, instruct students to count off from one to four (twenty-eight divided by seven). Then have all the number ones form a group, the twos another group, and so forth.

◇◇◇

Sometimes, such as during the early part of the school year or term, you may wish to have students work with friends of their choice in order to ensure that they will feel comfortable in the group. This plan can be followed easily by asking students to find two (or five, or ten) other students with whom to work. Be cautious though, since sometimes students may be reluctant to take the risk of choosing other members for fear of being turned down, or they may be hurt if they are not chosen by anyone.

◇◇◇

An alternative method of social grouping is the use of a sociometric device. Give each student a card and ask him to write his name in the upper left-hand corner and then to list two class members with whom he would like to work. Collect the cards and assign each student to a group in which there is at least one person he wants to work with, or in which one person has chosen him as someone he wants to work with.

◇◇◇

Interest grouping is another alternative that works well when there are a variety of tasks, ideas or problems. Allowing students to select the topic they are most interested in will often increase the initial involvement in the task. The card technique described above can be used for interest grouping as well as social grouping. Another grouping possibility is to use criteria like when birthdays fall (autumn, winter, spring, or summer) or what color clothing people are wearing (all the blues together, etc.). You can devise other grouping arrangements. Arranging for each student to work in many different kinds of groups will give you a chance to watch her operate with a variety of other students and make some judgments about how to group students for best results for different tasks.

LOOKING FORWARD

The next three chapters will further clarify implementation procedures. Chapter 6 considers the question, "What are the student skills needed for each structure?" The total role of the teacher is summarized in Chapter 7, and the question of how well each structure is working is considered in Chapter 8. At this point, you might find it helpful to skim through the Teacher Checklist at the beginning of Chapter 8 to review what has been covered in this chapter and get a preview of those things you will be looking for in your classroom as you implement the structures.

"achievement is a we thing,
not a me thing,
always the product
of many heads and hands..."

Atkinson 1974

student acquisition
of appropriate skills
learning with, against, and alone

INTRODUCTION

Once upon a time there were three students named Shadrach, Meshach, and Abednego. Shadrach was very concerned with being better than Meshach and Abednego. Whenever the teacher asked the three to work together, Shadrach would hide his own ideas and draw out the ideas of Meshach and Abednego. Shadrach would then secretly write his own report, taking pride that it was "better than" the group's report. This did not make Meshach and Abednego very happy. In fact, they began to refuse to work with Shadrach. Whenever the teacher said, "Would you three please work on this project together," Meshach and Abednego would say, "NO!" This did not make the teacher happy. Shadrach would just sit and smile and say, "I'm best!" After many failures to get Shadrach to cooperate with Meshach and Abednego, the teacher sought the advice of two wise educators. They suggested that perhaps Shadrach had never learned the skills needed to cooperate. "Teach Shadrach to be coopera-

tive," they suggested, "and his behavior will change." So the teacher did. And, not only did Shadrach's behavior change but Meshach and Abednego also learned how to cooperate more successfully.

This story illustrates an important point in using goal structures in your classroom. You now know how to structure instruction so that cooperative, competitive, or individualistic behavior by students is appropriate, but it does not follow that students will engage in cooperative, competitive, or individualistic behavior. The students must have the appropriate skills in order to respond to the goal structure implemented by the teacher. With each type of goal structure there is a set of skills each student needs to have mastered. Teachers often assume that students have the skills necessary to cooperate or compete with other students, or to work productively by themselves. This is often not the case, even when students are in high school and college. Family background and the nature of a student's peer groups influence the development of such skills. Many students come to school unable to work alone, to cooperate with others, or to compete successfully. To use successfully all three types of goal structures, teachers should deliberately teach the skills students need in order to engage in behavior appropriate to each type of goal structure and teachers should make sure that students perceive the goal structures correctly (see Chapter 8). They should also establish classroom norms and climate that support the use of the skills.

In this chapter we shall first discuss how students learn skills. We shall then discuss the skills a student needs in order to cooperate, compete, or function individualistically. Ensuring that students have the needed skills is an important first step in using goal structures in your classroom.*

HOW DO YOU TEACH SKILLS?

What is your role in teaching students skills? As the previous chapter indicates, one of the major reasons for monitoring students' behavior is to be able to identify the students who are having difficulties owing to missing or underdeveloped skills. Periodically you will want to review crucial skills with all your students. What are the steps you go through to ensure that students do learn cooperative, competitive, and individualistic skills?

---

* Students may at times overestimate their skill level and attempt behavior without really being able to do it. Once the younger of the two authors decided that he had the skills needed to beat up the older of the two authors (he was at the young and foolish age of three). He proceeded to demonstrate his skills the first time the older of the two authors made a face at him. Besides being cruelly humiliated, the younger of the two authors has had to look at his brother making faces at him for the past thirty-one years without being able to do anything about it.

Step 1: Ask the students what skills they think they will need in order to cooperate (compete, work individually) successfully. To be motivated to learn a skill, the students must see the need for the skill. If students do not suggest the needed skills, you will, of course, have to. But it is important to help students understand why they need the skill.

Step 2: Help the students get a clear understanding of what the skill is, conceptually and behaviorally. In order to learn a skill, the student must have a conception as to what the skill is and how the behaviors are executed. First the behaviors have to be identified and placed in proper sequence and in close succession. It is often helpful to demonstrate the skill, describe it step by step, and then demonstrate it again. Therefore, you need to be able to describe and do the skills being taught. Pointing out good models in other students is also useful. You might ask your students to identify someone in the class who has mastered that particular skill and can be used as a model.

Step 3: Set up practice situations. Once the skill is properly understood, the behavioral patterns need to be practiced until they are firmly learned.

Step 4: Ensure that each student receives feedback on how well he is performing the skill. Receiving feedback on performance is necessary in order to correct errors, identify problems in learning the skill, identify progress in skill mastery, and compare actual performance with the desired standard of performance. Feedback may be the single most important factor affecting the acquisition of skills. The more immediate, specific, and descriptive (as opposed to evaluative) the feedback, the more it will help skill development (see Johnson, 1972, for a full discussion of feedback). The better the advance conceptualization or understanding of the skill, the more helpful the feedback will be concerning the enactment of the behaviors involved in the skill. Feedback is often quite interesting to a student and increases his motivation to learn the skill. An important aspect of feedback is captured in rewarding students who successfully master the skill being taught. When students have been rewarded for skill mastery, they will tend to use the skills, and other students will imitate the behavior of rewarded students. It is not necessary that you provide feedback for every student. Dividing the students into cooperative groups in which they give each other feedback on skill performance is often just as effective.

Step 5: Encourage students to persevere in practicing the skill. In learning skills, students will need to persevere. The process of learning most skills involves a period of slow beginning, followed by a period of rapid gain, followed by a plateau in which performance does not increase, followed by another spurt of learning, followed by another plateau, and so on.

Plateaus are quite common in skill learning, and perseverance is necessary to keep one practicing until the next period of rapid gain begins.

After a series of classroom observations, anthropologist Jules Henry (1963) suggested that teachers encourage competition and criticism among students by modeling competitive behavior and rewarding it when it occurs—an observation that is consistent with existing research results (Bandura, Ross, and Ross, 1963). Since there is evidence that students are most likely to imitate the person with the greatest power and control over the distribution of rewards, the teacher's behavior will have a powerful influence on student behavior. In addition, a recent study by Masters (1972) indicates that if teachers offer an inequitable distribution of valued rewards to students, low-rewarded students are unlikely to be imitated. Thus, if a teacher models competitive behaviors and rewards students for engaging in competitive behaviors, the effect will be a great deal of competitive behavior on the part of most students.

Step 6: Set up situations in which the skills can be used successfully. Students need to experience success in skill development. It is their increasing sense of mastery that motivates further efforts to learn complex skills. If the skills are as necessary as the authors believe they are (and as research indicates), students will receive some reinforcement naturally as they begin to function more effectively within the goal structures.

Step 7: Require the skills to be used often enough so that they become integrated into the students' behavioral repertoires. A new skill must be integrated into a student's behavioral repertoire. It is at this stage that the performance of the skill becomes involuntary, automatic, and, finally, natural. After students have engaged in cooperative, competitive, and individualistic skills for a sufficiently long period, they will believe that the behavior is a natural response to the goal structure and will use the skills with little conscious awareness of doing so.

Step 8: Set classroom norms to support the use of the skills. Even if students master needed skills, they will not use them unless they believe that they are appropriate and supported. Johnson (1970) has a detailed discussion of how to establish classroom norms. Teacher modelling of the skills, the rewarding of students who appropriately engage in the skills, and the explicit statement of how you expect students to behave will influence the degree to which students engage in behavior appropriate to the goal structures.

Teacher Checklist for Student Skill Development

1. Do students believe the skill is needed and useful?

2. Do students understand what the skill is, what the behaviors are, what the sequence of behaviors is, and how it looks when it is all put together?

3. Have students had an opportunity to practice the skill?

4. Have students received feedback on how well they perform the skill? Was the feedback immediate, descriptive, and specific?

5. Have students persevered in practicing the skill?

6. Have students had the opportunity to use the skill successfully?

7. Have students used the skill frequently enough so that they have integrated the skill into their natural behavior?

8. Do the classroom norms support the use of the skill?

COOPERATIVE SKILLS

There are no skills more important to a human being than the skills of cooperative interaction. Most human interaction is cooperative interaction. Cooperation is the most important and basic form of human interaction, and the skills of cooperating successfully are the most important skills anyone needs to master. There is no way to overstate this point. Competitive and individualistic behavior cannot take place unless there is a broad cooperative framework in which persons are interacting. As stated previously, cooperation is the forest; competition and individualized effort are but trees.

Since almost all human behavior is cooperative, all interpersonal, group, and organizational skills can be identified as cooperative skills. It is impossible to list all such skills in this section, so we shall concentrate upon the more important and basic ones. Readers interested in a more thorough coverage of interpersonal and group skills are referred to Johnson (1972) and Johnson and Johnson (1975). The skills especially important for cooperation are communication skills, skills in building and maintaining trust, and controversy skills.

The Importance of Peer Tutoring

In most classrooms the resources of the students are seriously under-utilized under a rigid competitive or individualistic goal structure in which the teacher is supposed to teach each student. The opportunities for students teaching other students are lost. Yet there is considerable research that indicates that many students may learn better from their peers than from adults and that many students benefit greatly from teaching other students. Learning by some children is apparently inhibited when they are taught by what to them are giants or representatives of an alien adult world. Some children learn considerably better if they have the opportunity to learn from their peers. Communication may be more effective, amount of reinforcement may increase, and peer group encouragement may be more motivating when students teach each other. Although some students may be clumsy teachers at first, the research indicates that given practice and reinforcement for effective tutoring, most children can become rather good teachers.

COMMUNICATION SKILLS *

Communicating is the first step in cooperating †. Unless people can communicate with each other, they cannot cooperate. While it is very difficult to find a definition of communication with which everyone will agree, it is clear that *communication* is the exchange or sharing of thoughts and feelings through symbols that represent approximately the same conceptual experience for everyone involved. In emphasizing communication skills to students, it is possible to divide these skills into two categories, sending and receiving. Each student must be able to send messages that correctly represent her ideas, beliefs, feelings, opinions, reactions, needs, goals, interests, resources, and a host of other things; the skills needed to send these messages we will lump under "sending skills." Each student must also be able to receive messages accurately so he can understand the other person's ideas, beliefs, feelings, and so on; the skills needed to receive these messages we will lump under "receiving skills." Through sending and receiving, two students can clarify their mutual goals, plan how they are going to proceed to accomplish their goals, provide relevant information and intuitions to each other, reason together, coordinate their behavior, share their resources, give help and assistance to each other, and

---

* For a more complete discussion of communication and a series of exercises to increase communication skills, see Johnson (1972) and Johnson and Johnson (1975).

† Many of the misunderstandings between the authors when they were young stemmed from poor communication. Since the younger author didn't talk at all until about age four and then not so well, the older author needed to communicate in a more or less nonverbal manner.

spark each other's creativity. Thus it is upon sending and receiving skills that we shall focus in this section. What are important sending skills? The following are some of the most crucial (Johnson, 1973a).

1. *Clearly and unambiguously communicate your ideas and feelings.* Clearly "own" your message by (a) using personal pronouns such as "I" and "my" and (2) letting others know what your thoughts and feelings are. Students "disown" their messages when they use expressions such as "most people," "some people," "our group," making it difficult to tell whether the person really thinks and feels what he is saying or whether he is repeating the thoughts and feelings of others.

2. *Make your messages complete and specific.* Include clear statements of all necessary information that the receiver needs in order to comprehend the message. Being complete and specific seems so obvious, but often a person will not communicate the frame of reference he is taking, the assumptions he is making, his intentions in communicating, or the leaps in thinking he is making. Thus, while a person may hear the words he will not comprehend the "meaning" of the message.

3. *Make your verbal and nonverbal messages congruent with each other.* Every face-to-face communication involves both verbal and nonverbal messages. Usually these messages are congruent, so by smiling and expressing warmth nonverbally, a person can be saying that he has appreciated your help. Communication problems arise when a person's verbal and nonverbal messages are contradictory; if a person says, "Here is some information that may be of help to you" with a sneer on his face and in a mocking tone of voice, the meaning you receive is confused by the two different messages being simultaneously sent.

4. *Ask for feedback concerning the way in which your messages are being received.* In order to communicate effectively, you must be aware of how the receiver is interpreting and processing your messages. The only way to be sure is to continually seek feedback as to what meanings the receiver is attaching to your messages.

Being skilled in sending messages is only half of what is needed to communicate effectively; one must also have receiving skills. Receiving skills include providing feedback concerning the reception of another person's message; this feedback facilitates clarification and continued discussion. The major purpose for providing such feedback is to communicate one's desire to understand completely the ideas and feelings of the sender. The major barrier to effective communication is the tendency most people have to judge, evaluate, approve, or disapprove of the messages they are receiving. For instance, the receiver may respond nonverbally or openly with, "I think you're wrong," "I don't like what you said," "I think you're right," or "That is the greatest (or worst) idea I have ever heard!" Such evaluative receiving will make the sender defensive and cautious, thereby decreasing the openness of the communication. Thus, it is highly important for the receiver to indicate that he wants to understand the sender and will not evaluate the sender's messages until full understanding is reached. The specific receiving skills are paraphrasing, perception checking for feelings, and negotiating for meaning.

5. Paraphrase accurately and nonevaluatively the content of the message and the feelings of the sender. The most basic and important skill involved in receiving messages is paraphrasing. To paraphrase is to restate the words of the sender and it should be done in a way that indicates an understanding of the sender's frame of reference. The basic rule to follow in paraphrasing is, *You can speak up for yourself only after you have first restated the ideas and feelings of the sender accurately and to the sender's satisfaction.*

General Guidelines for Paraphrasing

1. Restate the sender's expressed ideas and feelings in your own words rather than mimicking or parroting her exact words.

2. Preface paraphrased remarks with, "You think . . . ," "Your position is . . . ," "It seems to you that . . . ," "You feel that . . . ," and so on.

3. Avoid any indication of approval or disapproval.

4. Make your nonverbal messages congruent with your verbal paraphrasing; look attentive, interested, and open to the sender's ideas and feelings, and show that you are concentrating upon what the sender is trying to communicate.

5. State as accurately as possible what you heard the sender say and describe the feelings and attitudes involved.

6. Do not *add* or *subtract* from the sender's message.

7. Put yourself in the sender's shoes and try to understand what it is he is feeling and what his message means.

---

6. Describe what you perceive to be the sender's feelings. Sometimes it is difficult to paraphrase the feelings of the sender if they are not described in words in the message. Thus a second receiving skill is the perception check for the sender's feelings. This check is made simply by describing what you perceive to be the sender's feelings. This description should tentatively identify the sender's feelings without expressing approval or disapproval of the feelings and without attempting to interpret or explain the causes of the feelings. It is simply saying, "Here is what I understand your feelings to be. Am I accurate?"

7. *State your interpretation of the sender's message, and negotiate with the sender until there is agreement on the message's meaning.* Often the words contained in a message do not carry the actual meaning. A person may ask, "Is it safe to drive this fast?" and mean, "Please slow down." A person may say, "That's a good suggestion," and mean, "I will ignore what you are saying and get rid of you by giving a superficial response." Sometimes paraphrasing the content of a message will do little to communicate your understanding of the message. In such a case, you negotiate the meaning of the message. You may wish to preface your response to the sender with, "What I think you mean is . . . ." If you are accurate, you then continue the discussion; if you are inaccurate, the sender restates the message until you can state what the esssential meaning of the message is. Keep in mind that it is the process that is important in negotiating meaning, not the actual phrasing you use. After the process becomes natural, a variety of introductory phrases will be used. Be tolerant of others who are using the same phrases over and over as they are developing this skill.

The sending and receiving skills described above seem very simple to most people. Yet they are very difficult to master fully and are indispensable when interacting with others. You should practice them consciously until they are as automatic as saying good morning.

Another element that has a great influence upon both communication and cooperation is the trust level within a relationship. It is to this issue that we now turn.

BUILDING AND MAINTAINING A TRUSTING CLIMATE

Why is trust important? Trust is a necessary condition for stable cooperation and effective communication. The higher the trust, the more stable the cooperation and the more effective the communication. Students will more openly express their thoughts, feelings, reactions, opinions, information, and ideas when the trust level is high. When the trust level is low, students will be evasive, dishonest, and inconsiderate in their communications. Students will more honestly and frequently declare their cooperative intentions and make contributions to a cooperative effort when they believe they are dealing with highly trustworthy individuals. Cooperation rests upon everyone's sharing resources, giving and receiving help, dividing the work, and contributing to the accomplishment of mutual goals. Such behaviors will occur when there is trust that all are contributing to the group's progress and are using their openness and resources for group rather than personal gain. The development and maintenance of trust is discussed at length in Johnson (1972); if possible, you should review the chapters on trust, self-disclosure, and acceptance before going ahead with this chapter.

◇◇◇

We rely heavily on a cooperative goal structure in our own university education classes, and have been impressed with the results. However, there are some unique problems at the university level. The major obstacle is that most of the students don't know each other, and therefore are not inclined to cooperate. When we walk into class for the first time, we see thirty individuals who are studiously ignoring each other except for a few scattered quiet conversations. The quietness seems unnatural, and our first job is to introduce the students to each other in a way that makes them comfortable. We often use things like the "informative nametag" where each student puts down his first name and also specified information in the corners of the cards (i.e., one corner might be places—where born? favorite?; another corner used for something unusual in the recent past and something you're looking forward to; etc.). Much of the first class period is spent in small informal conversations initiated by these name-tags, with instructions to get to know as many of these people as possible in the next half hour. This mixing and getting to know what other students have to offer to you (and you to them) needs consistent attention during the first few days of class and then seems to take care of itself. Other critical teacher responsibilities are the specifying and defining of the cooperative goal structure, the clarifying of the teacher's expectations, and the facilitating strategies des-cribed in Chapter 5.

◇◇◇

What is trust? Making a choice to *trust* another person requires the perception that the choice can lead to gains or losses, that whether you will gain or lose depends upon the behavior of the other person, that the loss will be greater than the gain, and that the person will likely behave so that you will gain rather than lose. Sounds complicated, doesn't it? There is nothing simple about trust; it is a complex concept and difficult to explain. Examples may help.

Trust is when you lend your older brother your bicycle; you may either gain his appreciation or lose your bike—which one happens depends upon him. You will suffer more if your bike is wrecked than you will gain by his appreciation, and you really expect him to take care of your bike! (Sad experience has led the younger of the two authors to recommend that you never lend your bike to your older brother.) For another example, con-sider this situation: A student is in a small group that is supposed to com-plete a report on the play *Macbeth*. The student begins to contribute to the discussion knowing that he will gain if he contributes good ideas that others accept and will lose if his ideas are laughed at and belittled. Whether he gains or loses depends upon the behavior of the other members of his group. He knows he will feel more hurt if he is laughed at than he will feel satisfaction if his ideas are appreciated. His expectation is that the other group members will consider his ideas and accept them. The issue of trust is expressed in the question every student asks: "If I openly express myself, will what I say be held against me?"

When student groups work on problem-solving tasks, what are the crucial elements of trust? Student cooperation requires openness and sharing, which are determined by the expression of acceptance, support, and cooperative intentions. *Openness* is the sharing of information, ideas, thoughts, feelings, and reactions to the issue the group is pursuing. *Sharing* is the offering of one's materials and resources to others in order to help them move the group toward goal accomplishment. *Acceptance* is the communication of high regard for another person and his contributions and behavior. *Support* is communicating to another person that you recognize his strengths and believe he has the capabilities needed to productively manage the situation he is in. *Cooperative intentions* are the expectation that you are going to behave cooperatively and that everyone else will also. From these definitions, *trusting behavior* may be defined as openness and sharing, and *trustworthy behavior* may be defined as expressing acceptance, support, and cooperative intentions. In assessing a student's trustworthy behavior, it is important to remember that accepting and supporting the contributions of other group members does not mean that one will agree with everything they have to say. A person can express acceptance and support the openness and sharing of others while at the same time expressing different ideas and opposing points of view. This is an important point in building and maintaining trust.

What is the teacher's role in initiating and encouraging trust among students during periods of cooperative activities? The following are some suggestions.

1. Encourage students to contribute openly their information, ideas, thoughts, feelings, intuitions, hunches, and reactions to the group's discussion and work.
2. Encourage students to share materials and resources.
3. Ensure that the students have the skills to express acceptance, support, and desire to cooperate.
4. Encourage students to express cooperative intentions, acceptance, and support toward each other during their cooperative interactions.
5. Point out rejecting and nonsupportive behaviors that shut off future cooperation, such as silence, ridicule, superficial acknowledgement of an idea.

6. Periodically have groups that are cooperating fill out the questionnaire on trusting and trustworthy behavior and discuss the results to see how their cooperation could be improved in the future.

Productive cooperation will exist within a group when members are both trusting and trustworthy; nonproductive cooperation will take place when group members are distrustful and untrustworthy. It is also possible for members of a group to be trusting but not trustworthy or to be trustworthy but not trusting. This pattern is represented as follows:

	High Acceptance and Support	Low Acceptance and Support
High Openness and Sharing	Trusting and trustworthy	Trusting, but untrustworthy
Low Openness and Sharing	Distrustful, but trustworthy	Distrustful and untrustworthy

EXAMINATION OF TRUST BEHAVIOR

In order to help you assess the level of trust within groups of students working cooperatively, a questionnaire is provided. This questionnaire may be reproduced and given to classes old enough to read or be used as a guide to interview students who cannot read at the necessary level. The procedure for using the questionnaire is as follows.

1. Have the students complete the questionnaire.
2. Have the students score the questionnaire.
3. Have the students discuss in their cooperative groups the way in which each member completed the questionnaire. Group members are to share their impressions of each other's trusting and trustworthy behavior. If such a discussion cannot take place, the students are to discuss the level of trust in the group indicated by such a lack of openness and feedback.
4. Instruct the students as to how they can skillfully build and maintain trust in their cooperative groups.

Remember that trust is appropriate only when individuals are cooperating. When they are competing, other skills are appropriate. The emphasis, therefore, should be placed on trust within a specific cooperative situation, not upon trust relationships in a wide variety of situations. Given below is the questionnaire. It is followed by instructions on scoring.

YOUR BEHAVIOR

Following are a series of questions about your behavior in the cooperative situation you have now completed (or are involved with). Answer each question as honestly as you can. There are no right or wrong answers. It is important for each student to describe his or her behavior as accurately as possible.

1. I offer facts, give my opinions and ideas, provide suggestions and relevant information to help the group discussion.
   Never   Seldom   Frequently   Always
2. I express my willingness to cooperate with other group members and my expectations that they also will be cooperative.
   Never   Seldom   Frequently   Always
3. I am open and candid in my dealings with the entire group.
   Never   Seldom   Frequently   Always

4. I give support to group members who are on the spot and struggling to express themselves intellectually or emotionally.

   Never   Seldom   Frequently   Always

5. I keep my thoughts, ideas, feelings, and reactions to myself during group discussions.

   Never   Seldom   Frequently   Always

6. I evaluate the contributions of other group members in terms of whether their contributions are useful to me and whether the other group members are right or wrong.

   Never   Seldom   Frequently   Always

7. I take risks in expressing new ideas and my current feelings during a group discussion.

   Never   Seldom   Frequently   Always

8. I communicate to other group members that I am aware of, and appreciate, their abilities, talents, capabilities, skills, and resources.

   Never   Seldom   Frequently   Always

9. I offer help and assistance to anyone in the group in order to bring up the performance of everyone.

   Never   Seldom   Frequently   Always

10. I accept and support the openness of other group members, supporting them for taking risks and encouraging individuality in group members.

    Never   Seldom   Frequently   Always

11. I share any materials, books, sources of information, or other resources I have with the other group members in order to promote the success of all members and the group as a whole.

    Never   Seldom   Frequently   Always

12. I often paraphrase or summarize what other members have said before I respond or comment.

    Never   Seldom   Frequently   Always

13. I level with other group members.

    Never   Seldom   Frequently   Always

14. I warmly encourage all members to participate, giving them recognition for their contributions, demonstrating acceptance of and openness to their ideas, and generally being friendly and responsive to them.

    Never   Seldom   Frequently   Always

To score this questionnaire, count "Never" as 1, "Seldom" as 2, "Frequently" as 3, and "Always" as 4. √ Reverse the scoring on questions 5 and 6. Then add the scores in the following way.

Openness and Sharing		Acceptance and Support	
1. _____		2. _____	
3. _____		4. _____	
√ 5. _____		√ 6. _____	
7. _____		8. _____	
9. _____		10. _____	
11. _____		12. _____	
13. _____		14. _____	
Total _____		Total _____	

If a student has a score of 21 or over, classify him as being trusting or trustworthy, whichever the case might be. If a student has a score of under 21, classify him as being distrustful or untrustworthy, whichever the case might be.

<><><><><><><><><><><><><><><><><><><><><><><><><><><><><><><><><><><><><><>

Tutoring Skills

In order to provide help and assistance to fellow cooperators a student needs to learn:

1. How to recognize that he needs help

2. How to ask others for help

3. How to search for others who may need assistance

4. How to provide instruction, feedback, and reinforcement for other students

Such skills can be easily learned through a series of role-playing situations developed by the teacher.

<><><><><><><><><><><><><><><><><><><><><><><><><><><><><><><><><><><><><><>

CONTROVERSY SKILLS *

When students working cooperatively are openly sharing their ideas, information, reactions, intuitions, resources, and materials, differences and disagreements will surface. *Such inevitable controversies are a necessary condition for creative insights and productive work in a cooperative situation, especially in complex problem-solving situations.* A controversy is a

* For a more detailed and complete discussion of controversy and exercises for building controversy skills, see Johnson and Johnson (1975).

discussion, debate, or dispute in which opinions clash. Every decision contains potential controversy, as a decision is a choice among alternative courses of action. When communication is effective, when trust is high, cooperators will find themselves in disagreement and will engage in a discussion or debate to determine which assumptions, ideas, information, or course of action to adopt and follow. In order to function effectively within a cooperative goal structure, students will have to have skills in promoting and managing constructive controversies. To an effective cooperative group, controversy means that the members' ideas need to be drawn out more, more information needs to be obtained, and group thinking needs to be reexamined.

What student skills should teachers emphasize to promote the constructive management of controversies?

1. *Define controversies as problem-solving situations in which differences need to be clarified, rather than as "win-lose" conflicts in which one person's ideas have to dominate.* Destructive controversies are characterized by an orientation on the part of students to "win" at the expense of other group members whose ideas are defeated. In a "win-lose" situation, every action is seen in terms of who is going to dominate whom. Such a competitive orientation within a cooperative situation will seriously undermine cooperation. When controversy is approached from a problem-solving point of view, students tend to recognize the legitimacy of each other's ideas and contributions and search for a solution accommodating the needs of all group members.

2. *Be critical of ideas, not persons.* Ideas are discussed, not personalities, and nothing personal is meant in disagreement. It is possible to express disagreement without being personally rejecting, and students should be encouraged to do so. This is an important skill for cooperators to learn.

3. *Appropriately pace differentiation (bringing out differences) and integration (putting the different ideas together) phases of the problem-solving process.* First, all different points of view are brought out and explored. Second, creative syntheses to arrive at the best solution are sought. It is a serious mistake to look for ways to integrate ideas before all the differences have been explored. *The potential for integration is never greater than the adequacy of the differentiation already achieved.*

4. *Take the point of view or perspective of other students so you understand what they are saying from their frame of reference.* This procedure, sometimes called role reversal, is a skill that everyone must master. It is the ability to understand how a situation appears to other students and how they are reacting cognitively and emotionally to the situation. It is crucial for integrating different perspectives into a more complete and higher quality solution to the problem being worked upon. The opposite of such perspective taking, *egocentrism,* is the inability to take another person's perspective.

◇◇

Many of the controversy skills are promoted by inquiry learning situations. There is a strong relationship between inquiry teaching and cooperation; inquiry tasks are problem-solving situations and a cooperative goal structure is generally the most appropriate one to use. The question-asking strategies, brainstorming of alternatives, open discussion of ideas, and other aspects of inquiry teaching will all help in resolving controversies. Other suggestions for inquiry teaching are:

1. Initiate controversy in order to increase student interest and motivation. Sharpening up students' ideas, opening up new possibilities, deepening the level of analysis and insight, can all be accomplished by teachers when they initiate controversies.

2. Reward the posing of alternatives (which will increase controversy) by students.

3. Reward students for changing their minds when confronted with evidence (this is an important behavior for teachers to model).

4. Encourage students to consider alternatives from different points of view (the story of the three blind men and an elephant is always a good example of the value of perspective taking).

◇◇

COMPETITIVE SKILLS

Competition, when it is appropriate, is fun and adds spice to classroom life. Because competition involves much less interaction among students and much less coordination of behavior, there are fewer skills essential to competing.

The major competitive skill students need to learn is that of monitoring the progress of competitors to know how they are doing. Since winning is the goal of competition, the only way to know where one stands is to know where the others are. A teacher can promote the development and use of monitoring skills by:

1. Making clear that monitoring is part of the competition and that students can watch each other's progress

2. Setting up several methods of monitoring including charting students' progress on the board, checking periodically to bring everyone up to date, clustering students together

3. Joining in the competition occasionally in order to model the active interest in others' progress necessary for monitoring and the enjoyment possible from competing (win or lose)

A second competitive skill involves clarifying the rules before the competition begins and then following them. Each student needs to know what can and cannot be done in the competition. In some competitions, students are allowed to enhance their chances of winning by making it more difficult for their opponents to win (e.g., "sending" another player's ball away from the wicket in croquet). In other competitions, such disruption of opponents' progress would be declared unfair (e.g., cutting in too soon in a track race results in being disqualified). If the rules are clear in the beginning, student behaviors will usually be appropriate. If any student feels it is necessary to break the rules, the situation is probably inappropriate for competition (e.g., he perceives that the goal is too important and the situation too serious).

What about the student who has to win all the time? A student who competes inappropriately presents a problem for a teacher because he can cause competitive reactions on the part of other students in cooperatively and individualized situations. Experience in all three goal structures and specific attention to cooperative skills for that student may end inappropriate competition. What about the student who refuses to compete? After experiencing all three goal structures, most students realize that competition can be enjoyable. One way of finding out if students enjoy competition is to make competitions voluntary; if a number of students do not choose to compete in a situation, it could mean either that competition is inappropriate or they do not perceive the conditions as appropriate for competition.

Two aspects of competing a teacher may wish to be sensitive to are (1) overgeneralizing the outcome of any one competition (e.g., if a student loses a footrace she should not think of herself as being generally a "loser") or (2) being a poor winner or loser. Students need to develop appropriate attitudes in which they can win or lose gracefully and with good humor, and in which they can look at the results of any one competition as limited information on which to base their worth. Using competition only in appropriate circumstances will go far toward encouraging these perspectives.

INDIVIDUALISTIC SKILLS

Individualized instruction should be used when there are specific skills or a specific series of facts to be mastered. Since there is no interaction with other students in an individualized situation, learning under such a goal structure requires the fewest skills. Each student needs his own materials, enough space to be isolated from others, and a clear understanding of what he is supposed to do. The primary skill necessary is to be able to work on one's own, ignoring other students (i.e., not being distracted or interrupted by what other students are doing).

Besides being able to "tune out" the world, students need to assume responsibility for task completion and for evaluating their own progress. Charts and records are often used to help students evaluate themselves. Successfully answering questions about the content of what one is reading is an example of self-evaluation in an individualized learning situation. Completing a task on one's own depends on the amount of importance one assigns to mastering the material. The importance will probably be greatest when the results of the individualized learning are to be contributed to a group problem-solving project in which the student is working cooperatively with others. Having one's fellow students depend upon you for certain skills or facts increases the motivation to master them.

GO

SCIENCE CLASS

EXPERIMENT IN GROUPS

MATH CLASS

TOURNAMENT IN TEAMS

★ GATHER 30 STUDENTS
AND
MOVE PAST GO

INDIVIDUAL RESEARCH FOR THEME

ENGLISH CLASS

SEVEN

are you ready?
putting it all together

INTRODUCTION

The preceding chapters have dealt with the problems of structuring (i.e., setting up the appropriate classroom structure for what you want to do). Are you ready to try it in the classroom? Select an instructional sequence, preferably one you are actually going to teach. Now work through the following questions with that specific instructional sequence in mind. (It may help to have a piece of paper and a pencil handy. You may be able to use it as your lesson plan when you finish.)

WHAT IS YOUR ROLE AS THE TEACHER?

1. *Specify the desired outcomes; cognitive and affective outcomes you want students to acquire from the lesson or unit should be specified in*

advance. What should students be able to *do* as a result of this experience? What should they be able to *say?* How should they *feel?*

You may want to review the charts in Chapter 2 concerning possible outcomes. Although you should have an idea of what you want to have happen as a result of each activity, don't get too hung up here. Common mistakes we make are specifying too many desired outcomes and being locked in too tightly to the outcomes we specify.

◇◇◇

Once there was a slightly strange psychologist who wanted to teach pigeons how to play Ping-Pong and rabbits how to dance. One day while he was working with his rabbits, his apparatus broke down. When he returned to his rabbits a few days later, all that they remembered of the dance was the first part, a kind of hop. The rabbits found this a very valuable way to move about and have been hopping ever since.

Moral: Unplanned and unexpected outcomes may be more interesting than planned outcomes. So don't get so blinded by expected outcomes that you can't see the very worthwhile and interesting unexpected ones.

◇◇◇

2. *Select the appropriate goal structure to implement.* Would a cooperative structure work best? Why? Would an individualistic structure work best? Why? Would a competitive structure work best? Why?

Review Chapter 4 for help in selecting a goal structure to fit your desired outcomes. Consider both the cognitive achievement of the students and their affective growth. In almost every situation, one structure will work better than either of the others.

◇◇◇

In a classroom, much like yours and ours, a teacher was attempting to get a number of students (too many, of course) to solve a difficult problem. Each student was working alone, and *the teacher urged each child to be the first to solve the problem.* The students worked hard, knowing that the kind of grade they got depended on their solving the problem before the other students. They felt pressured and frustrated. Suddenly, as the students were trying to work at their task and keep an eye on the other students at the same time, a hand shot into the air. One could almost hear the sigh of disappointment (and relief?) from the other students. With the pressure to be first gone, some of the students returned to the problem in a more relaxed frame of mind and others unobtrusively gave up. Many of the students felt some resentment and dislike for the student who had finished first (again) and were rationalizing to themselves that they didn't really like this subject anyway (or the teacher, either).

Moral: When students are faced with a problem-solving task under a competitive structure, not only do they achieve less but they are described as aggressive, oppositional, obstructive, and self-defensive. In terms of the anxiety level, students were reported to be more anxious, less self-assured, showing more incidences of self-oriented needs, less able in recitation, and dissatisfied with discussion. This report is not so much an indictment of competition as a description of what can happen when a goal structure is used inappropriately.

◇◇◇

3. *Arrange the classroom and instructional materials to promote the implementation of the goal structure.* Do students need to work in clusters or individually? Are the materials appropriately distributed? Are materials to be shared or does each student have his own set? Do the students have enough space?

Review Chapter 5, pages 77–78 for help. The most frustrating example of inappropriateness here is when students are expected to work individually but have to share materials. Space to work in is also important.

4. *Communicate the learning goal to the students.* Is the goal a group or individual goal? Does the group have a single product or does each student have a product? What are the rewards for reaching the goal? Should the students' work be rewarded on the basis of a fixed set of standards, or should it be rewarded on the basis of how it compares to the work of other students?

Review Chapter 5, pages 79–82 for help. Remember that using different goal structures in different situations is new not only to you but also to the students. The cooperative goal structure will be especially difficult for students with standard school backgrounds. Make their understanding of the goal structure clear.

5. *Communicate what students can expect from each other (student–student interaction).*

6. *Communicate what students can expect from you (teacher–student interaction).* Are students expected to work together or alone? Do students monitor each other's work or ignore each other? Is a division of labor possible or is each student expected to do the entire task? Do students turn to each other for help, or to the teacher?

Review Chapter 5, pages 82–85 for help. Remember that you have to behave consistently with the goal structure you have selected, and see that the students do also.

As we were visiting some teachers in a small elementary school, we noticed several children trying to jump rope in a small room that served as a gym when the regular gym was being used by another class. There was extreme frustration as ropes became tangled and walls hindered the jumping. After a few moments of this confusion, one large rope was set up and a line was formed to jump one at a time. As we then moved down the hall, we couldn't help thinking how nice it would have been to have had a larger space so that the students in that long line could have improved their skill in jumping and practiced while waiting for a turn on the larger rope.

Moral: Facilities do make a difference on goal structuring. The individualistic structure especially needs enough room (and materials) for students to spread out and work on their own.

7. *Check signals with students for such things as "get started," "Things are getting a little too boisterous," "I need your attention for a moment," "Clean up,"* and so on.

8. *Facilitate appropriate student behavior by monitoring the classroom, intervening (when necessary) to improve classroom processes, and modelling and praising appropriate behavior.* Are you the primary resource for the students? What behaviors are you encouraging? Do the students have the required skills to engage in these behaviors? How do you monitor the progress? How do you monitor the goal structure?

Review Chapters 5 and 6 for help, and then read Chapter 8 on monitoring. After you have answered the points listed above, you are ready to

implement the goal structure. After the goal structure is implemented, you must monitor student behavior to ensure its appropriateness (if students start competing in a cooperative situation, your anticipated learning outcomes will not result). How you monitor student behavior is discussed in the next chapter.

9. *Evaluate results and communicate the evaluation to students, parents, school personnel, and other interested people.* Did students achieve the desired outcomes under this goal structure? What else was achieved? What is the best way to report results; and to whom?

◇◇◇

Musings of a teacher: "I'm sure I set the goal structure up perfectly. What went wrong? I explained the goal structure and made my expectations clear. I had the room arranged appropriately, and the goal structure is the one which best fits the outcomes I wanted. So why didn't those outcomes appear? I must have done something wrong!"

Moral: Conscientiously setting up the appropriate structure for what you want to do does not ensure success, it's only a very good start. Other variables, such as the difficulty of the task, the interpersonal relationships in the classroom, and the preceding student experiences, will also have an effect on the learning outcomes.

◇◇◇

Last but most important is the appropriate way to regard the evaluation process. These observed outcomes are the reason we structured things the way we did, the reason this curriculum was written, the reason you are being paid. However, don't try to cramp all the outcomes down into the knowledge (what students can say after it's over) bag. The most important outcomes are the cognitive and affective skills learned that can now be used in many different situations. Measuring more than just the knowledge aspect of the situation is difficult. Read Chapter 9 carefully for advice in this area.

◇◇◇

"Just doing it was so much work that I've forgotten why I did it."

Anonymous teacher, on evaluation

◇◇◇

EIGHT

monitoring your classroom
listening, watching,
and reflecting

WHY MONITOR?

Imagine that you have conscientiously gone through the steps of implementing a goal structure; does that mean that optimal student learning will automatically result? The answer is no. Because of misunderstandings, lack of skills, inexperience, or bad habits, students may not behave appropriately, and the potential effect of the goal structure may be lost. Students may compete when they are supposed to be cooperating, they take a competitive activity too seriously and become too concerned over the results, or they may decide to talk about football instead of doing an individualized lesson. So after you implement the appropriate goal structure, you must monitor the classroom to ensure that classroom organization, student-student interaction, and teacher-student interaction are appropriate to the goal structure being used. In other words, besides being skillful in implementing the goal structures, you need to develop a sensitivity toward how effectively

121

it is operating! Through observation and questionnaire procedures, you may obtain the information needed to determine whether appropriate activities are taking place and what sorts of interventions (if any) you should initiate to improve the congruence between the goal structure and classroom processes.

There are several ways to monitor your classroom after you have implemented a goal structure. It may seem impossible to use all the procedures suggested, but with a little bit of practice you will be surprised how easy it is to use the procedures contained in this chapter. The methods of monitoring classroom processes we discuss are:

1. Teacher role checklist
2. Teacher observation of classroom organization and student-student interaction
3. Observation by another person (student or aide) of teacher-student interaction
4. Teacher observation of student cooperative skills
5. Anecdotal observation by teacher
6. Student perception questionnaire

After monitoring classroom processes, reflect on the information gathered and make a judgment as to whether an intervention is needed to improve the congruence between the goal structure and what is taking place within the classroom. If any intervention is needed, you then implement it and continue monitoring to see if the problems have been corrected.

"The teacher turns to the class and says, 'Well, who can tell Boris what the number is?' There is a forest of hands and the teacher calls on Peggy who says that 4 should be divided into both the numerator and denominator. It is obvious that Boris's failure made it possible for Peggy to succeed, and, since the excited handwaving of the children indicates that they wanted to exploit Boris's predicament to succeed where he was failing, it appears that at least some of the children were learning to hope (covertly) for the failure of fellow students."

Jules Henry, 1963

TEACHER ROLE CHECKLIST

The first step in monitoring classroom processes is to identify the teacher behaviors necessary to implement each goal structure. In Chapter 5 we began a discussion of such behaviors. The description of the teacher's role in Chapter 7 provides additional help in defining what the teacher should do to implement successfully each goal structure. The following checklists provide the basis for verifying that you have gone through the necessary steps to set up successfully the goal structure best suited for your instructional purposes. There is a separate checklist for each goal structure. After implementing a goal structure for a specific lesson, it may be helpful to go through the appropriate checklist and make notes on how students are behaving. Such review will help increase your skill in implementing the three goal structures.

TEACHER ROLE CHECKLIST FOR COOPERATIVE INSTRUCTION

1. What are the desired outcomes for the problem-solving activity?
   a. Cognitive outcomes:

   b. Affective outcomes:

2. Is the classroom arranged so that students:
   _____ are clustered together in groups and focused on each other and on shared instructional materials?
   _____ have access to each other, can approach each other, and can talk with each other?
   _____ share materials such as books and equipment with little duplication (unless the subject matter requires it) of materials among group members?

3. Have you effectively communicated to the students that:
   _____ the instructional goal is a group goal (each group produces a single product)?
   _____ each group will be rewarded on the basis of quality or quantity of group output according to a fixed set of standards?

4. Have you effectively communicated the expected patterns of student-student interaction? Are students aware that they should:
   _____ interact with each other?
   _____ share ideas and materials and help each other in any way possible?
   _____ work in groups, pool their information and resources, divide up the task so that different students do different parts when it is

desirable, and integrate each member's work into a group product?

_____ perceive teacher praise, support, or criticism as a reflection on the whole group, not just on one or more members?

_____ demonstrate cooperative skills by being attentive to the other members of their group, accepting their comments and actions with expressions of friendliness and warmth, genuine attempts to understand, encouragement for further contributions, and clarification of points of view?

_____ offer suggestions to move the group towards its goal, make direct verbal attempts to influence the group to move towards goal accomplishment, support efforts to accomplish goals by clarifying, questioning, restating, and summarizing, and use plural pronouns such as "we," "us," and "our"?

_____ seek help and assistance from group members, not the teacher?

5. Have you effectively communicated the expected patterns of teacher-student interaction? Do students know that the teacher:

_____ wants them to work with other students in a group to create a group product and will evaluate them on the basis of how their group product matches a fixed set of standards?

_____ will observe groups, serve as a consultant to stimulate thinking, will not give the solution to the problem, will provide assistance to the group as a whole, and will give emotional support for group effort?

_____ will praise and support students working together for goal accomplishment, sharing ideas and materials, dividing up the work, and utilizing each other's resources to combine their efforts?

TEACHER ROLE CHECKLIST FOR INDIVIDUALIZED INSTRUCTION

1. What are the desired outcomes for the activity of learning specific knowledge and noncomplex skills?
   a. Cognitive outcomes:

   b. Affective outcomes:

2. Is the classroom arranged so that students:

   _____ are isolated at separate desks or by a seating arrangement that separates them as much as possible?

   _____ are arranged to do their own work without approaching or talking with each other?

   _____ have individual sets of self-contained materials?

3. Have you effectively communicated to students that:

   _____ the instructional goal is an individual goal (each student masters the material on his own)?

_____ each student will be rewarded on the basis of how his work meets a fixed set of standards for quality and quantity?

4. Have you effectively communicated the expected patterns of student-student interaction? Do students know that they:

_____ should not interact with each other?

_____ should work on the assignment alone, trying to ignore completely the other students?

_____ should perceive teacher praise, support, or criticism of another student as totally irrelevant to their own mastery of the assigned material?

_____ should ignore comments from other students?

_____ should go to the teacher for all help and assistance needed?

5. Have you effectively communicated the expected patterns of teacher-student interaction? Do students know that the teacher:

_____ wants them to work by themselves and to master the assigned material without paying attention to other students, and will evaluate them on the basis of how their efforts match a fixed set of standards?

_____ will interact with each student individually, setting up learning contracts, viewing student progress, providing assistance, giving emotional support for effort, and answering questions individually?

_____ will praise and support students for working alone and ignoring other students?

TEACHER ROLE CHECKLIST FOR COMPETITIVE INSTRUCTION

1. What are the desired outcomes for the drill activity?

    a. Cognitive outcomes:

    b. Affective outcomes:

2. Is the classroom arranged so that students:

_____ are clustered together, working on their own, but able to monitor the progress of their competitors?

_____ have access to each other only if (1) it is required by the nature of the competition or (2) to know whether they are ahead or behind the others?

_____ have an individual set of self-contained materials?

3. Have you effectively communicated to students that:

_____ the instructional goal is an individual goal (each student produces her own product)?

_____ each student will be rewarded on the basis of how her work compares to the work of the other students in the cluster?

4. Have you effectively communicated the expected patterns of student–student interaction? Do students know that they should:

_____ interact only to check the progress of other students?

_____ work on the assignment alone, trying to do the task better, faster, and more completely than the other students?

_____ perceive teacher praise or support of another student's work as an indication that their own work is inferior and teacher criticism of another student's work as an indication that their own work is superior?

_____ ignore comments from other students?

_____ go to the teacher for all help and assistance needed?

5. Have you effectively communicated the expected pattern of teacher–student interaction? Do students know that the teacher:

_____ wants each student to try to do better on the assignment than the other students and will evaluate work on the basis of how it compares with the work of other students?

_____ will interact with each cluster of students—clarifying rules, clarifying the task without giving one student more help than another, and often making clarifications to the entire class?

_____ will praise and support students working alone and trying to do better, faster, and more work than any other student in the cluster or classroom?

STRUCTURED OBSERVATION SCHEDULES

While students are working on their learning tasks, the teacher or an observer may monitor the situation through the use of the observation schedules given below. There will be many times when you are too busy to make the observations you need, so it is helpful to train students, an aide, the principal (yes, we did say principal), or another teacher to use the schedules. The appropriate procedure follows.

1. Allow a few minutes for the activity to get started. Select the time you are going to allow between observations (five minutes, seven minutes, or ten minutes).

2. Go through the questions at a steady pace, checking the appropriate box for each question and writing in comments freely, including notes on overheard conversations and student behaviors that are representative and interesting. Don't let the commenting keep you from completing the schedules. Five minutes should be considered enough time for completing all three schedules. You may find yourself distracted by the be-

* Additional observation forms may be found in Johnson and Johnson (1975).

havior of one or more students. *Keep in mind that your primary target is the behavior of the majority of the students, and notes on divergent behaviors should be clearly labelled as such.*

3. When you have completed the schedules, wait for the beginning of the next time period and then repeat the procedure. Many of the observations may not have changed and can just be checked again. You should get through the schedules several times during each observation period.

4. When the observation period is over, add the number of checks indicating cooperative, competitive, or individualized instruction. Then convert to percentages through the procedure given on page 138.

Table 8-1 Frequency of Use of Each Goal Structure

Module	Monday	Tuesday	Wednesday	Thursday	Friday
1					
2					
3					
4					
5					
6					
7					
8					
9					
10					

In the table above, mark the subject area focused upon (reading, science, etc.) and the goal structure used. At the end of the week, it will be possible to determine what percentage of the time each type of goal structure was used; the time, or period, during the day when certain goal structures were used; and which goal structures were used with certain instructional tasks.

It is important that you as the teacher get considerable experience in using these observation schedules. As you become skillful in observing classroom processes, you will become more aware of the different aspects of the goal structures and will be able to watch students more closely and pick up appropriate comments and behavior. You will also be better able to train other observers for your classroom. With frequent use of the schedules, you will be able to observe classroom activities automatically while at the same time interacting with students.

CLASSROOM ORGANIZATION OBSERVATION INSTRUMENT

This observation checklist is to help you observe the classroom organization relevant to cooperative, competitive, and individualistic learning. For each question note the alternative that best describes the existing classroom organization. Then put an x in the appropriate box of the alternative selected. Each box represents a new observation (observations can be made every five, seven, or ten minutes). Whenever possible, write in comments about the situation, but don't let the commenting keep you from completing the checklist. Do not be distracted by incongruencies in the classroom organization; keep in mind that your primary target is to observe the overall classroom organization.

1. **How would you describe the learning situation?**

   ☐☐☐☐☐☐☐☐☐   a. Problem solving

   ☐☐☐☐☐☐☐☐☐   b. Specific factual knowledge or noncomplex skill development

   ☐☐☐☐☐☐☐☐☐   c. Drill

2. **How are students arranged for the learning task?**

   ☐☐☐☐☐☐☐☐☐   a. Students are clustered together in groups so that they can focus on each other and on shared instructional materials.

   ☐☐☐☐☐☐☐☐☐   b. Students are isolated from each other through separate desks or by a seating arrangement that separates them as much as possible so that they can work on their own set of learning materials without distractions.

   ☐☐☐☐☐☐☐☐☐   c. Students are clustered together so that they are able to work alone but can still monitor the progress of the others.

   ☐☐☐☐☐☐☐☐☐   d. There is no set arrangement; students are clustered together or are isolated at tables or desks; students have a variety of focuses.

3. **How accessible are students to each other during the learning task? The room is organized so that:**

   ☐☐☐☐☐☐☐☐☐   a. Students have access to each other, can approach each other, and can talk with each other.

⬚⬚⬚⬚⬚⬚⬚⬚⬚ b. Students are arranged so they can do their own work without approaching or talking with each other.

⬚⬚⬚⬚⬚⬚⬚⬚⬚ c. Students have access to each other only if (1) it is required by the competition or (2) to check to see whether they are ahead or behind the others.

4. How accessible are the materials needed for the learning task? The room is organized so that:

⬚⬚⬚⬚⬚⬚⬚⬚⬚ a. Students share materials such as books and equipment with little duplication of materials among group members (unless the subject matter requires it).

⬚⬚⬚⬚⬚⬚⬚⬚⬚ b. Each student has a self-contained set of materials.

5. Diagram the classroom, indicating the arrangement of students, their access to materials, and their interaction patterns.

STUDENT-STUDENT INTERACTION

This observation checklist is to help you observe student-student interaction relevant to cooperative, competitive, and individualistic learning. For each question note the alternative that best describes the present interaction among students. Then put an *x* in the appropriate box of the alternative selected. Each box represents a new observation (observations can be made every five, seven, or ten minutes). Whenever possible, write in comments about the situation, but don't let the commenting keep you from completing the checklist. Do not be distracted by the behavior of individual students; keep in mind that your primary target to observe is the behavior of the majority of the students.

1. Are most students interacting with each other?

   ☐☐☐☐☐☐☐☐☐ a. Many students are interacting with each other.

   ☐☐☐☐☐☐☐☐☐ b. Almost no student interaction is taking place.

   ☐☐☐☐☐☐☐☐☐ c. Only the checking of other students' progress is taking place.

2. What type of interaction is taking place?

   ☐☐☐☐☐☐☐☐☐ a. Students are sharing ideas and materials, and helping each other.

   ☐☐☐☐☐☐☐☐☐ b. Students are working on the task alone, trying to ignore other students completely.

   ☐☐☐☐☐☐☐☐☐ c. Students are working on the task alone, but they check to see where other students are on the assignment; there is no copying, sharing, or helping.

   ☐☐☐☐☐☐☐☐☐ d. Most students are interacting with each other in a social way, ignoring the task to be completed.

3. What method are students using to accomplish the assigned task?

   ☐☐☐☐☐☐☐☐☐ a. Students are working in groups, pooling their information and resources; where desirable they are dividing up the work so that different students do different parts, and they are integrating each student's work into a group product.

   ☐☐☐☐☐☐☐☐☐ b. Students are working alone, trying to complete the task and ignoring other students.

☐☐☐☐☐☐☐☐☐   c. Students are working alone, each trying to do the task better, faster, and more completely than the other students.

4. What is the reaction of students when one member of their cluster receives praise, support, or criticism from the teacher?

☐☐☐☐☐☐☐☐☐   a. Students' verbal and nonverbal behaviors indicate that they perceive teacher praise, support, or criticism as a reflection on the whole group, not on just one or two members.

☐☐☐☐☐☐☐☐☐   b. Students' verbal and nonverbal behaviors indicate that they perceive teacher praise, support, or criticism of another student as totally irrelevant to their own accomplishment.

☐☐☐☐☐☐☐☐☐   c. Students' verbal and nonverbal behaviors indicate that they perceive teacher praise of another student as an indication that their own work is inferior and perceive teacher criticism of another student as an indication that their own work is superior.

5. How attentive are students to fellow students?

☐☐☐☐☐☐☐☐☐   a. Students are attentive to other members of their group and accept their comments and actions with expressions of friendliness and warmth, genuine attempts to understand, encouragement for further contributions, and clarification of points of view.

☐☐☐☐☐☐☐☐☐   b. Students attempt to ignore comments from other students.

6. Are the students group oriented or self-oriented in achieving task?

☐☐☐☐☐☐☐☐☐   a. Students offer suggestions to move the group toward its goal, make direct verbal attempts to influence the group to move toward goal accomplishment, support efforts to accomplish goals by clarifying, questioning, restating, summarizing, use "we," "us," "our," and other plural pronouns.

☐☐☐☐☐☐☐☐☐   b. Students are intent on achieving task for themselves, ignoring other students.

☐☐☐☐☐☐☐☐☐   c. Students are intent on achieving task for themselves, checking progress of other students so that they can do better.

7. From whom do the students seek help and assistance?

☐☐☐☐☐☐☐☐   a. Students seek help and assistance from each other.

☐☐☐☐☐☐☐☐   b. Students go to the teacher for all assistance and help.

TEACHER-STUDENT INTERACTION

This observation checklist is to help you observe teacher–student interaction relevant to cooperative, competitive, and individualistic learning. For each question note the alternative which best describes the present interaction between the teacher and the students. Then put an *x* in the appropriate box of the alternative selected. Each box represents a new observation (observations can be made every five, seven, or ten minutes). Whenever possible, write in comments about the situation, but don't let the commenting keep you from completing the checklist. Do not be distracted by unusual teacher behaviors; keep in mind that your primary target is to observe what the teacher is doing a majority of the time with a majority of the students.

1. Has the teacher communicated to the students that:

☐☐☐☐☐☐☐☐   a. They are supposed to work with other students in a partnership to create a single group product and that they will be evaluated on the basis of how the group product matches a fixed set of standards?

☐☐☐☐☐☐☐☐   b. They are supposed to work by themselves to master the assigned material without paying any attention to other students and that they will be evaluated on the basis of how their efforts match a fixed set of standards?

☐☐☐☐☐☐☐☐   c. They are supposed to work by themselves to do better on the assignment than other students and that they will be evaluated on the basis of how their work compares to the work of the other students?

2. What is the pattern of teacher-student interaction?

☐☐☐☐☐☐☐☐   a. Teacher observes groups, serves as a consultant to stimulate thinking of group members, will not give the solution to a problem, provides assistance to the group as a whole, gives emotional support for group effort.

☐☐☐☐☐☐☐☐☐   b. Teacher interacts with each student individually, setting up learning contracts, viewing progress, providing assistance, giving emotional support for effort, answering questions individually.

☐☐☐☐☐☐☐☐☐   c. Teacher interacts with each cluster of students—clarifying rules, clarifying task without giving one student more help than another, settling disputes, and often making clarifications to entire class.

☐☐☐☐☐☐☐☐☐   d. Teacher interacts with no one; teacher is working alone at his desk, out of the room, observing at a distance.

☐☐☐☐☐☐☐☐☐   e. Teacher interacts with entire class through lecturing, answering individual questions in front of entire class, giving instructions to entire class,

3. What student behaviors does the teacher encourage by praise, criticism, and example?

☐☐☐☐☐☐☐☐☐   a. Teacher praises and supports students who work together for goal accomplishment by sharing ideas and resources, dividing up the work when it is appropriate, and utilizing each other's resources to combine their efforts.

☐☐☐☐☐☐☐☐☐   b. Teacher praises and supports students for working alone and ignoring other students.

☐☐☐☐☐☐☐☐☐   c. Teacher praises and supports students working alone and trying to do better, faster, and more work than any other student in the cluster or classroom.

After you use the observation schedules a few times, you may not need the extensive explanation contained in the original instruments, and you may be able to get by with the short form.

SHORT FORMS OF THE OBSERVATION SCHEDULES

Classroom Organization

Learning Situation	Problem solving											
	Specific knowledge or skill											
	Drill											
Student Arrangement	Clustered—sharing											
	Isolated											
	Clustered—comparing											
	No set arrangement											
Student Access to Each Other	Open access											
	No access											
	Comparing access											
Student Access to Materials	Sharing—little duplication											
	Self-contained set											

Student-Student Interaction

Student Interaction	Much interaction												
	Almost no interaction												
	Only comparing												
Type of Interaction	Sharing and helping												
	Working alone—ignoring												
	Working alone—comparing												
	Social												
Method of Accomplishing Task	Pooling—division of labor												
	Working alone—focus on task												
	Working alone—doing better												
Reaction to Praise and Criticism	Generalized to whole group												
	Irrelevant												
	Superior-inferior feelings												
Attending	High attending												
	Ignoring—disregarding												
Orientation	Group oriented												
	Self-oriented—ignoring												
	Self-oriented—doing better												
Assistance	Each other												
	Teacher												

Teacher-Student Interaction

Goal Instruction Group produce—fixed standards														
Individual product—fixed standards														
Individual product—comparison														
Pattern of T-S Interaction T consults with groups—facilitates														
T gives specific answers to individuals														
T clarifies rules—settles disputes														
T does not interact														
T interacts with whole class—lectures														
T. Support T supports sharing, helping, combining														
T supports working alone—ignoring														
T supports working alone—doing better														

SCORING THE STRUCTURED OBSERVATION SCHEDULES

From the structured observation schedules a summary can be made representing the percentage of time that cooperation, individualization, and competition were reflected in the classroom arrangement, the student-student interaction, and the teacher-student interaction. The procedure for determining the percentage for each observation schedule is as follows.

Classroom organization:

1. Find the total possible score by multiplying the number of times you were able to go through the complete schedule (range from 1 to 10) by 4 (the number of questions in the schedule).

   Total Score _____

2. Count the number of cooperative, individualistic, and competitive responses to the questionnaire.

   Cooperative: 1a, 2a, 3a, 4a   Total _____
   Individualistic: 1b, 2b, 3b, 4b*   Total _____
   Competitive: 1c, 2c, 3c, 4b*   Total _____
   Other: 2d   Total _____

3. Find the percentage by dividing the number of responses for each goal structure by the total possible number.

   Cooperative percentage   = _____
   Individualistic percentage = _____
   Competitive percentage   = _____
   Other percentage   = _____
   Total percentage   = 100%

◇◇◇

Let's try an example. Step one: I was able to get through the schedule 5 times which is multiplied by 4 to give me a total score possibility of 20. Step two: I count 10 cooperative checks, 5 individualistic checks, and 5 competitive checks. Step three: The percentages are found by dividing 10 (the cooperative scores) by 20 (the total possible scores) for .50 or 50%. Repeating this for the individualistic scores (5 divided by 20) and the competitive scores (5 divided by 20) will give me .25 or 25% for each. That should add up to 100%.

◇◇◇

  * This response can be scored as either individualistic or competitive, but it cannot be scored as both! Use it for one or the other, depending upon the goal structure you are implementing.

Student-Student Interaction:

1. Following the same procedure, find the total possible score by multiplying the number of times you were able to go through the complete schedule (range 1 to 10) by the number of questions in the schedule (7).

    Total Score _____

2. Count the number of cooperative, individualistic, and competitive responses to the questionnaire.

    Cooperative: 1a, 2a, 3a, 4a, 5a, 6a, 7a   Total _____

    Individualistic: 1b, 2b, 3b, 4b, 5b*, 6b, 7b*   Total _____

    Competitive: 1c, 2c, 3c, 4c, 5b*, 6c, 7b*   Total _____

    Other: 2d   Total _____

3. Find the percentage by dividing the number of responses for each goal structure by the total possible score.

    Cooperative percentage   = _____
    Individualistic percentage = _____
    Competitive percentage   = _____
    Other percentage   = _____
    Total percentage   = <u>100%</u>

◇◇

Another example? After observing a baboon troop in their natural habitat, we can get the baboon-baboon interaction patterns by multiplying the number of times we got through the schedule (10), by the number of questions (7) to get a total possible score of 70. The second step is to count the actual number of cooperative, individualistic, and competitive alternatives noted (i.e., back-scratching, flea picking, banana peeling, and mate finding). We count 40 cooperative checks, 10 individualistic checks, and 20 competitive checks from the observation schedule. (We realize it was difficult to follow subjects to the tops of some of the trees.) In the third step, we find that the cooperative percentage for the group is 57% (40 divided by 70), the individualistic percentage is 14% (10 divided by 70), and the competitive percentage is 29% (20 divided by 70). Even though it appears that the baboon troop is more cooperative than many of our classrooms, we discourage further comparisons between baboons and students. (Some students have suggested that baboon behaviors may also be observed in colleges of education.)

◇◇

* This response can be scored as either individualistic or competitive, but it cannot be scored as both! Use it for one or the other, depending on the goal structure you are implementing.

Teacher-Student Interaction:

1. Following the same procedure, find the total possible score by multiplying the number of times you went through the schedule (range 1 to 10) by the number of questions (3).

Total Score _____

2. Count the number of cooperative, individualistic, competitive, and other alternatives checked on the questionnaire.

Cooperative: 1a, 2a, 3a   Total _____
Individualistic: 1b, 2b, 3b   Total _____
Competitive: 1c, 2c, 3c   Total _____
Other: 2d, 2e   Total _____

3. Compute the percentages by dividing the number of responses for each goal structure by the total possible score.

Cooperative percentage   = _____
Individualistic percentage = _____
Competitive percentage   = _____
Other percentage   = _____
Total percentage   = 100%

◇◇◇

Now you try it. You were able to go through the schedule five times, and you have five checks for 1c, five checks for 2c, and five checks for 3a. What do the percentages look like? What advice do you have for this teacher? Perhaps before you give advice, you had better consider all three schedules.

◇◇◇

The overall picture of the classroom is perhaps more important than the results from any one of these three schedules. To get an overall percentage for each structure, you average the percentages across all three observation schedules.

1. Add percentages for:

classroom organization cooperation, student-student cooperation, and teacher-student cooperation percentages   Total = _____
classroom organization individualistic, student-student individualistic and teacher-student individualistic percentages   Total = _____
classroom organization competition, student-student competition and teacher-student competition percentages   Total = _____

It is profitable to take a few minutes after you have organized the data to ponder just what the results mean. One way is to make three or more true statements from the data. Consider the following example.

The data indicate that:

1. I am a super teacher.

2. My students are a little slow and have trouble perceiving things correctly.

3. In terms of the classroom, I have nothing to work with and nobody to go to.

2. Divide each score by 3 to get average.
   Cooperation average percentage   = _____
   Individualistic average percentage = _____
   Competition average percentage   = _____

At this point, you can begin to see how consistently the goal structures are being implemented and develop some suggestions for improving them. However, keep in mind that you don't have the student perceptions of what is going on in the classroom.

OBSERVING COOPERATIVE SKILLS

In addition to observing student-student interaction, it may be helpful to observe the use of the cooperative skills. On page 142 is an observation sheet focusing on cooperative behaviors. For each time period, write the initials of the group members who use the skill. Time periods may be for five, seven, or ten minutes (coordinate with the student-student interaction schedule). If you see cooperative behaviors not listed on the observation sheet, write them in at the bottom and note the frequency of their occurrence. *It will be very helpful for students if they are trained in the use of this observation sheet and if, every day, one student is given the responsibility of observing group work and reporting the frequency with which each group member uses the skills!* In order to maximize the learning of cooperative skills by students, make sure that each student has frequent experience in observing cooperative behaviors in a group of peers.

COOPERATIVE SKILLS OBSERVATION SHEET

			Time									
COMMUNICATION — Sending	"Owns" message											
	Describes thoughts											
	Describes feelings											
	Contributes idea, suggestion											
COMMUNICATION — Receiving	Asks for feedback											
	Paraphrases											
	Describes others' feelings											
	Negotiates meaning											
	Describes effect of others											
TRUST	Expresses warmth, liking											
	Expresses support, acceptance											
	Expresses cooperative intentions, motivation											
CONTROVERSY	Emphasizes mutual problem											
	Criticizes ideas, not persons											
	Differentiates											
	Integrates											
	Other											
	Other											

ANECDOTAL OBSERVATION: EAVESDROPPING

The use of structured observation schedules is not the only way to observe classroom processes, and further explication of observation procedures is given in Chapter 9. As long as you are hearing or seeing the class, you are monitoring. Informal, off-the-cuff observation is always taking place; the challenge is to become aware of it and make it as accurate and helpful as possible. The first step is to make your unconscious monitoring conscious.

We have a great deal of respect for the intuition of an experienced teacher, and if you haven't already done so, you should learn to tune in on your intuitive hunches. Yet more powerful information than intuition about students' learning is possible to get, even with tight schedules, demanding students, and ringing bells. In this section we shall focus on observing incidents in the classroom in ways that allow you to record them and go back over them and reflect on their implications, thereby keeping an accurate record of student behavior so you can document changes and recognize growth in a student.

Becoming more precise in your natural monitoring of students in the classroom is called eavesdropping. *Eavesdropping* is the recording of significant, specific events involving students, and it enables you to answer such questions as, "What are the students doing when they aren't working with me?" and "What are the students saying when they aren't talking with me?" The emphasis is on the significant, and it is not necessary to record an observation for each student each day; five or six significant observations during a school day would be doing very well, and some days may not provide any. The characteristics of good eavesdropping are that observations are *specific*, they don't degenerate into generalities, they are brief enough to be written down quickly, they capture an important aspect of the behavior of one or more students, and they provide help in answering questions about the successful implementation of goal structures or the progress of students.

Eavesdropping differs from the more systematic observing strategies presented in this chapter and in Chapter 9 in that it is concerned primarily *not* with quantitative information (such as how many times or what percentage of the time) but with qualitative incidents (such as conversations or behaviors of unusually high interest), which may occur somewhat infrequently. When both systematic observation and eavesdropping are used well and simultaneously, most of the relevant information from your classroom is available to you.

We really do not do enough eavesdropping. Even though we continually monitor, when do we feel we have the time to watch, listen, and *record?* We seem to catch a glimpse here and a comment there as we rush from thought to thought doing our best to see that an assignment is valuable for everyone. Of course, every once in a while something happens in the classroom that is unusual enough to cause us to stop teaching and notice, but if we don't write it down, we have an anecdote that changes drastically by the second time we've told it. By beginning to jot down the significant events gathered by our natural monitoring, we can learn to eavesdrop skillfully.

How do you learn to be in the right place at the right time? Actually, there are significant things going on all around you, and being in the right place is not as important as tuning in on what you are seeing and hearing. Probably the largest obstacle is the habit that students have of stopping what they are doing whenever a teacher is near and waiting expectantly for the teacher to talk. We usually oblige, don't we? Your first task in eavesdropping is to be able to join a group of students, or an individual student, without saying anything. The second task is to systematize the procedure of watching and listening so that it becomes habitual, and the third task is to follow through on the observations so that they are useful. For effective eavesdropping, consider the following advice.

1. *Time:* You have to make time (*plan for it*) every so often to step back and watch, listen, and record for a minute. None of the goal structures requires you to be in the "limelight" all of the time. You will need to develop the habits of taking the time to become aware of what you are observing and of recording your observations in a systematic way.

2. *Recording procedures:* It *is* necessary to record your observations if you are to maximize their benefit. For one thing, your memory of what took place changes as you try to recall classroom events. New observations quickly get assimilated into old stereotypes and impressions of students. The sharpness of detail and completeness of the situation are rapidly lost as your mind becomes attentive to new events. You need to develop a style of recording that allows you to make a permanent record of an incident as it is taking place. A stenographer's notebook, a few three-by-five-inch index cards in a pocket, a small tape recorder, or scratch paper can facilitate the immediate recording of observations.

3. *Organizing and Reflecting Time:* You will want to get as much mileage from your observations as possible. Take fifteen minutes at the end of the day to read through what you have recorded. The anecdotes you have collected become valuable as you reflect on their significance. In such reflection do not confuse your observations with your inferences! You observed what was actually said or done; inferences come later, as you interpret the student behavior and reflect on its "whys" and "purposes." It is also helpful to organize your eavesdropping around such questions as, "How well are the goal structures functioning?" and "How are students responding to the three different goal structures?" The structured observation schedules will provide you with a cognitive framework within which to organize the results of your eavesdropping.

4. *Make a Permanent Record:* You will find many uses for a permanent record of the anecdotes you collect. Write your anecdotes in a log or other information-keeping device so that you may review them periodically to see what changes are taking place within the classroom and so that you may communicate to parents and other interested parties what students are doing in your classroom. At the end of each evaluation period, a number of anecdotes about each student is of importance in clarifying what at level student performance is. Some teachers even make

it a point to call parents each week to share some positive student behavior with them. This habit pays dividends by promoting a cooperative spirit between the teacher and the parents. How often do most parents get calls from teachers with something good to share about their child? Try it!

STUDENT PERCEPTIONS

In establishing whether or not the goal structure being used has been implemented successfully, an important question to ask is, "Do students understand how they are supposed to behave?" Such student understanding is achieved by using the questionnaire, "What We Are Supposed To Do." At the time you use the questionnaire, you will have already eavesdropped on student discussions and used the formal observation checklists. You may also wish to interview individual students, to join in the activities occasionally, and to check the perceptions of the clusters verbally. This questionnaire, however, will prove valuable in your monitoring of student behaviors.

The method of administering the questionnaire will vary according to your situation. Some students will be able to take it on their own at the beginning of an instructional activity. In other classes, you may want to read the questions aloud or question a few representative students on a one-to-one basis. With young students, some of the questions may need to be rephrased. How often you use the questionnaire depends on how experienced you and your students are in using the different goal structures and on whether you feel that you need the information. It is always helpful to sample student perceptions.

STUDENT PERCEPTION QUESTIONNAIRE: WHAT WE ARE SUPPOSED TO DO

Complete the following questionnaire by marking the alternative that best describes what you are supposed to do during the learning session about to begin.

1. On this assignment we are supposed to:
   _____ a. Work with other students in partnerships to create a single group product.
   _____ b. Work by ourselves to create individual products, without paying any attention to other students.
   _____ c. Work by ourselves to create individual products better than any other student's work.

2. The teacher will give out grades, points, praise, or other rewards on the basis of:

   _____ a. The quality of group work according to a fixed set of standards.

   _____ b. The quality of individual work according to a fixed set of standards.

   _____ c. The quality of individual work according to how it compares with the work of other students.

3. The teacher wants us to:

   _____ a. Work together on the task, sharing ideas and materials, and helping each other.

   _____ b. Work on the task alone, trying to ignore other students completely.

   _____ c. Work on the task alone but check to see where other students are on the assignment, without copying, sharing, or helping.

4. The teacher wants us to:

   _____ a. Work in groups, pooling information and resources, dividing up the work when it is desirable so that different students do different parts, and integrating each student's work into a group product.

   _____ b. Work alone, trying to complete the assignment to the best of our ability, while ignoring other students.

   _____ c. Work alone, each trying to do the task better, faster, and more completely than the other students.

5. Check one of the following:

   _____ a. I am pleased and happy when the teacher praises the work of one of the students in my group, as it means we are doing well.

   _____ b. It makes no difference to me one way or the other when the teacher praises the work of another student, as it is irrelevant to my own accomplishment.

   _____ c. I am unhappy when the teacher praises the work of another student, as it indicates that my work is inferior.

6. Check one of the following:

   _____ a. Helping other students in my group to complete their work will help my chances for getting a good grade.

   _____ b. Helping other students to complete their work will not affect my chances for getting a good grade one way or another.

   _____ c. Helping other students to complete their work will hurt my chances for getting a good grade.

7. The teacher wants us to:

   _____ a. Be attentive to other members of our group, to be interested in what they have to say, and encourage the participation of all members.

   _____ b. Ignore the comments of other students, as they will interrupt my work.

_____ c. Ignore the comments of other students, as they will decrease my chances of winning.

8. The teacher wants us to:

_____ a. Seek help and assistance from other students in our group when we need it.

_____ b. Seek help and assistance from the teacher when we need it.

9. The teacher wants us to:

_____ a. Use the cooperative skills of effective communication, trust building, and productive controversy.

_____ b. Use the individualistic skills of assuming responsibility for personal task completion and evaluation of progress and "tuning out" the rest of the students.

_____ c. Use the competitive skills of trying to win, keeping track of whether I am ahead or behind other students, and following the rules.

10. Check: either (a.) or choose between b., c., or d.:

_____ a. I like doing the assignment in this way.

(or)

_____ b. I would rather be working with other students in a partnership to complete the assignment.

_____ c. I would rather be working alone to complete the assignment.

_____ d. I would rather be trying to do the assignment better than any of the other students.

SCORING THE STUDENT PERCEPTION QUESTIONNAIRE

From the results of the student perception questionnaire ("What We Are Supposed To Do"), a summary can be made representing the percentage of students who have understood the goal structure being implemented. The procedure for summarizing the results of the questionnaire is as follows:

1. Find the total possible score by multiplying the number of students by 9 (omitting Question 10): Total possible score = _____

2. Count the number of cooperative, individualistic, and competitive responses to the questionnaire.

    Cooperative: 1*a*, 2*a*, 3*a*, 4*a*, 5*a*, 6*a*, 7*a*, 8*a*, 9*a*   Total _____

    Individualistic: 1*b*, 2*b*, 3*b*, 4*b*, 5*b*, 6*b*, 7*b*, 8*b**, 9*b*   Total _____

    Competitive: 1*c*, 2*c*, 3*c*, 4*c*, 5*c*, 6*c*, 7*c*, 8*b**, 9*c*   Total _____

* This response can be scored as either individualistic or competitive, but it *cannot* be scored as both! Use it for one or the other, depending upon the goal structure you are implementing.

3. Find the percentage by dividing the number of responses for each goal structure by the total possible score:
Cooperative percentage   = _____
Individualistic percentage = _____
Competitive percentage   = _____
Total percentage   = 100%

4. Tabulate the results of Question 10:
Percentage preferring cooperation   = _____
Percentage preferring individualized = _____
Percentage preferring competitive   = _____
Total percentage   = 100%

◇◇

Do you remember how to do this from the observation schedules? Try this score-sheet from a sixth grade individualized math class. We interviewed ten students and got the following responses:

Question	Student Responses	Question	Student Responses
1 a.	0	6 a.	0
b.	10	b.	9
c.	0	c.	1
2 a.	0	7 a.	7
b.	8	b.	3
c.	2	c.	0
3 a.	6	8 a.	5
b.	2	b.	5
c.	2	9 a.	0
4 a.	0	b.	10
b.	10	c.	0
c.	0	10 a.	2
5 a.	2	b.	6
b.	8	c.	0
c.	0	d.	2

Note: You should remember that Question 10 is separated from the other nine questions and needs special interpretation. Flip back to page 147 and read Question 10 again. Knowing what goal structure is being implemented along with the student perception data from the other nine questions, you can interpret from question 10 what the student prefers.

Response 10a has a corollary in b, c, or d so that if the student likes the present structure and it is individualistic, he should also prefer 10c and it would not be marked. As you can see, that is what happened in this case. If 10a is not marked in an individualistic setting, then the cooperative (10b) or competitive (10d) choice is likely to be marked. These ten students showed a strong preference for cooperation.

◇◇

MONEY-BACK GUARANTEE

Are you sick of observing? Does figuring percentages get you down? Have the students stolen all your pencils and has your electronic calculator run down from overuse? Do you wake up in the middle of the night yelling "total cooperative is 47 percent!" Do you want to rip this chapter out of the book and forget it? Do you want to throw the entire book in the wastebasket and forget it? * Before you do, consider the Johnson and Johnson remedy.

The Johnson and Johnson remedy guarantees that if you consistently use these monitoring procedures until they become automatic and unconscious, your teaching will become easier, more effective, and more enjoyable. If it does not, you can send this book along with a description of how it has failed to the younger of the two authors for your money back. The reason why it is so important to observe the classroom situation systematically is that it is quite common for teachers to misjudge completely the consistency of specific behaviors of students. You need sensible ways to gather information that tells you whether your implementation of goal structures is working and documents your efforts for interested administrators and parents. In addition, just as students react to feedback concerning their performance as reinforcing, you will react to documented evidence concerning the effectiveness of your behavior as reinforcing. It is highly satisfying to look at the records and see a marked and steady increase in the effectiveness of your goal structuring.

PUTTING IT ALL TOGETHER

It is helpful to summarize the results of the structured observation schedules and the student perception questionnaire in a way that allows direct

---

* The younger of the two authors once tried to throw the older of the two authors into a wastebasket and forget him. Consequently, the younger of the two authors ended up wearing the wastebasket on his head for several days. The younger of the two authors now is easily recognized by his wastebasket-shaped head.

and easy comparison. Figure 8-1 is constructed for that purpose. For this task you need three colors of ink: blue for cooperative percentages, green for individualistic percentages, and red for competitive percentages.

Look at Figure 8-1 and read through these directions before you start. On the Classroom Organization Observation Schedule line (the first line), plot the percentage points for each structure (cooperation, competition, and individualistic). Repeat the procedure on the Student-Student Interaction Observation Schedule line, Teacher-Student Interaction Observation Schedule line, and Student Perception Questionnaire line. Now connect all the cooperation points across the page using the blue ink. Do the same for individualistic (in green) and competition (in red). This will give you feedback on how consistent the selected goal structure is. Is the classroom organization consistent with student-student and teacher-student interaction? How do the perceptions of the students coincide with the observed structure? Do the plotted lines ever cross? Why?

FIGURE 8-1   *Summary of Observation and Questionnaire Percentages*

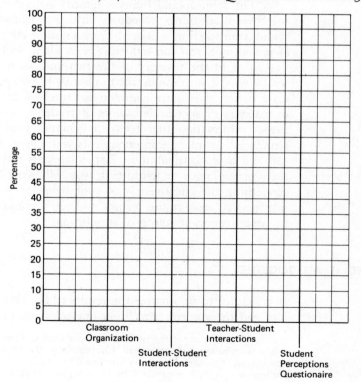

We have plotted the percentages from a classroom we have observed. Look at the chart and see if it helps make the procedure clear and if you can make some statements about this instructional situation from the data (i.e., almost no competition present in the goal structure).

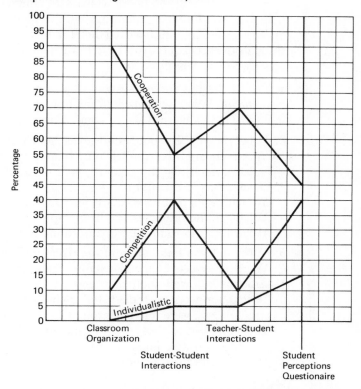

TEACHER REFLECTION

After accumulating the information from monitoring several lessons, you have lots of information. What should you do with it? (Not so fast with that wastepaper basket suggestion.*) The information can do a lot for you, and probably has already contributed to your skill at goal structuring. Monitoring will make you more aware of the variables involved in goal structuring and provide you with the information you need to increase your goal-structuring skills.

* The younger of the two authors once suggested to his older brother what he could do with his observations of the younger one's behavior. Ever since that day the younger of the two authors has listened carefully and respectfully to any and all of the older brother's observations of and reflections on the younger brother's behavior!

In order to benefit from the information you have collected, you need to reflect on it. Some time spent looking over the results of the monitoring will help you shape up those loose ends and make your classroom truly cooperative, industriously individualistic, and excitingly competitive. To help you, the following questions are included in this chapter. Reflecting on these questions has proved helpful to other teachers. Thinking back through the procedures you have learned about in this chapter, what kinds of answers can you give?

1. For the lessons you monitored, what goal structures did you wish to implement? What percentage of the time do you use for each? Cooperative _____, individualistic _____, competitive _____, unspecified _____.

2. What did you find out from the teacher checklist?
   Was there anything you left out? If so, why?
   What interesting things did you do that were not included on the checklist? Add them to it!
   Which goal structure is easiest for you to implement?
   What are the problems you have implementing each goal structure?
   What ideas do you have for your future use of each goal structure?

3. What did you find out from the structured observation schedules?
   Were all aspects of the classroom organization congruent with the goal structure you were implementing?
   Were all aspects of student-student interaction congruent with the goal structure you were implementing?
   Were all aspects of teacher-student interaction congruent with the goal structure you were implementing?
   How did the three types of observations compare with each other? (See Figure 8-1.)
   What ideas do you have for your future use of each goal structure?

4. What did you find out from your anecdotal observations?
   Were your observations consistent with the results of the structured observation schedules?
   How would you summarize your anecdotes?
   How do students seem to react to each type of goal structure?
   What were the most distinctive anecdotes?
   What ideas do you have for your future use of each goal structure?

5. What did you find out from the student perception questionnaire?
   Do students correctly perceive what they are supposed to be doing?
   Are there any aspects of cooperating, working individually, or competing that the students do not correctly perceive?
   What goal structure do students prefer? (See Question 10.)
   How do the results of the questionnaire compare with the results of the observations? (See Figure 8-1.)
   What ideas do you have for your future use of each goal structure?

6. General reflection questions:

Are the goal structures clear to the students? Do the students understand what they are supposed to be doing?

How effective was I in matching goal structures with desired processes and outcomes?

Are students engaging in the necessary kinds of behaviors?

Am I engaging in the necessary kinds of behaviors?

Am I and are the students improving in our ability to function within each of the goal structures?

Do students have the necessary skills to function within each of the goal structures?

What could I be doing to facilitate the goal structures even further?

Am I encouraging, modelling, and rewarding the appropriate behaviors? During the average school day, what percentage of the time are the students spending within each goal structure? Cooperative _____, individualistic _____, competitive _____.

INTERVENTIONS TO CORRECT PROBLEMS

Once the information gathered in the monitoring procedures has been recorded in Figure 8-1 and examined, you may decide that certain modifications are needed to promote greater congruence between the goal structure being used and the classroom processes.

Problems may stem from:

1. Your own actions. (For example, you may have failed to make clear to students what the goal structure is, and what your expectations are for student-student interactions.)

2. Lack of student skills. (For example, students may not know how to communicate with each other, thereby decreasing the effectiveness of cooperative goal structures.)

3. Inexperience of the students. (For example, they may not be able to cooperate without constant emphasis by the teacher on the importance of cooperating.)

4. Incorrect use of goal structures. (For example you may be asking students to compete when the goal is so important that the negative consequences of competition arise.)

Once the problem is clear, the modification necessary to correct it is usually also clear. When in doubt, show the results of the monitoring data to the students and use a cooperative goal structure to promote student planning on how to correct the situation. Often just the awareness of the recorded information (for example, telling a group that they are not sharing and helping) will get them back on the right track.

report
card

To Parent:

This is a report of work and progress.
Our schools wish to develop each pupil
to the limit of his capacity
that he may make the most of himself
and contribute the greatest good to society.
Citizenship, character, service, and loyalty—
knowledge, skills, attitudes, and appreciation
are our goals.
Home and school must work together.
We are here to serve you and yours.

Sincerely yours,

Superintendent

NINE

evaluating outcomes
and communicating results
what has happened
and who needs to know?

INTRODUCTION

Once upon a time there were two happy teacher educators who went around to schools telling teachers all the wonderful things they could now do with their students. Many teachers were impressed by what the educators had to say, and they began to do the things the educators recommended. Interested in what was taking place, the principal, parents, and potential employers of students came to watch what the teachers were doing. Soon everyone was asking the teachers questions.

"All this is fine," said the principal, "but how do you give students grades? I will have to fire you if you don't give students grades every six weeks!"

"All this is fine," said the parents, "but how much are my children learning? I will go to the school board and have you fired if my children aren't learning!"

"All this is fine," said the employer, "but will the students be good workers? If your students don't turn out to be good workers, I will not hire any and then you will be fired!"

"All this is fine," said the students, but how do we know whether we need to improve or not? If you do not tell us how well we are doing, we will riot and then you will be fired!"

So the teachers went back to the happy educators and said, "All this is fine. But how do we evaluate our students while we do it?"

"That's an important issue," said the teacher educators, "Here is our answer."

This story illustrates the need to be concerned about the evaluation of students any time new instructional procedures are suggested. The purpose of this book is to make teaching easier, more productive, and more enjoyable by improving the teacher's relationships with his students, improving the processes of learning and the classroom climate, and increasing the achievement of desired cognitive and affective outcomes. The basic thesis of this book is that through the appropriate use of all three goal structures this purpose will be accomplished. In Chapter 1 we stressed that goal structures are the most important instructional variable in the classroom and that the teacher can have more impact upon learning and classroom life through appropriately using the goal structures than through engaging in any other set of behaviors. In Chapter 2, we presented the results of considerable research to validate these points. The appropriate use of goal structures is a path to achieving desired educational outcomes. Every teacher has responsibilities that are broader than instruction, and one such broader responsibility is evaluation. No matter how effective or how much fun a new instructional practice is, teachers will want to know how they are to assign grades (i.e., evaluate student performance) when using the new procedure. In discussing this issue, we shall first review the purposes and nature of evaluation and then detail procedures to use for evaluation when appropriately using the three goal structures.

WHY IS EVALUATION OF OUTCOMES IMPORTANT?

Evaluation is one of the hardest and most unpleasant activities teachers are required to engage in. Very few teachers like to give tests, score papers, or assign grades. Yet evaluation is necessary, and it can be helpful to the teacher, student, school, and society. What is evaluation? *Evaluation* is the process by which judgments are made concerning the merit of a particular performance. In evaluating, the crucial question is, "Are the desired educational outcomes being achieved?" The answer to this question is necessary to determine the success of the instructional program and to determine the student's progress toward educational goals. There are many ways in which evaluations made by teachers are used! Here are some of the more important ones.

1. Instructional Program Guidance. Both expected and unanticipated outcomes of instruction should be measured if a teacher is to make judgments concerning what to do next or what to repeat the next time the subject is taught. Evaluations are useful in identifying areas of strength and weakness so that instructional programs can be modified and improved. The revision and improvement of instructional programs depend upon competent evaluation. The instructional program consists of the goal structures being used, the materials provided to students and teachers, the behavior of teachers, the effectiveness of the support given to teachers and students by administrators and special services, the methods of instruction used, and so on. Through evaluation, the components of the instructional program can be revised and reorganized to be more effective.

2. Information on Instructional Program Success. Evaluations can provide information on the success of the instructional program to administrators, parents, publishers, school boards, potential employers of students, government officials, college admission officers, and so on. There are many reasons why it is important for society to have information on the success of instructional programs of schools.

3. Student Guidance. Evaluations provide information to students about their success in school, as a whole, or in a specific instructional unit. Such evaluations are useful in identifying areas of strength and weakness so that student performance can be modified and improved. In order to make informed choices about what courses to take, skills to practice, material to review, the student needs to know on what level he is performing. Persons interested in the student's future (such as parents and counselors) also need evaluations of student performance in order to provide informed counsel as to what future educational and occupational opportunities the student should seek out and apply for. Basic to our democratic philosophy is that opportunities be available on the basis of competency (as opposed to family background or membership in an elite group), so information about competency is vital.

4. Information on Student Success. Besides persons interested in counseling students, others who need information on student success in instructional situations include college admission officers, potential employers, and administrators and teachers of schools a student is transferring to. They should receive information about a student's competence in order to ensure that important decisions about future opportunities of students are made on the basis of such competence rather than on the basis of sex, ethnic background, social class, or heredity. (There is an important issue as to whether many of the current measures of competence favor some groups within our society and are biased against other groups, but that issue will not be discussed here.)

5. Administrative Purposes. Evaluations are useful for making all sorts of administrative decisions (which again are supposed to be made on the basis of competence, not privilege), about such things as student promotions, transfers, placements, graduation, and selection for honors. Administrators in most schools also need to make decisions about retraining, promoting, rewarding, and rehiring school personnel. Modifying materials, changing class sizes, initiating changes in teachers' schedules and patterns of interaction (such as team teaching), and other aspects of improvement of instruction require administrative decisions. Competent evaluation is needed to provide valid information to the administrators who make such decisions.

◇◇◇

Teachers evaluate all the time! Deciding to stay with one activity or go on to something else, deciding who is good in reading and who is good in math, deciding to cut one period short or prolong a discussion, deciding to repeat a set of lessons or to skip another set altogether—all these moment-to-moment and day-to-day decisions are based upon intuitive evaluations. Intuition in good teachers is usually a pretty accurate means of decision making. But every teacher finds it helpful to collect specific information, to make it possible to explain to others why certain decisions were made and to check up on his intuition.

◇◇◇

Perhaps the final reason why evaluation of outcomes is important to teachers is that everyone seems to be interested in having teachers do it. Teachers, students, parents, administrators, school boards, and many more groups and individuals want to know the results of such evaluations. Each group has a preconceived notion as to what should be evaluated, how the evaluation should be conducted, and how the results should be reported. Since every group is looking at the situation from a different perspective or frame of reference, there are always differences of opinion on what evaluational activities the teacher should be engaging in. Ultimately it is up to the teacher to do the evaluations. If for no other reason than to keep everyone else off their backs, teachers need to be concerned about valid evaluations of students and instruction.

Before presenting the procedures that should be used to evaluate students while using flexibly all three goal structures, we shall first review the ways in which cognitive and affective outcomes can be measured. If you do not need such a review, skip to page 165.

COGNITIVE OUTCOMES

In Chapter 2 we reviewed a series of cognitive outcomes that are affected by the type of goal structure being used. Most of these cognitive outcomes deal with the achievement of the student in learning the information, procedures, and skills the teacher focuses upon in instruction. Other cognitive outcomes deal with skills involved in interacting with other students. Some of the cognitive outcomes mentioned are mastery of factual material, mastery of assigned skills, mastery of concepts and principles, verbal abilities, writing abilities, competence in cooperative, competitive, and individualized work, problem-solving success, self-awareness, and ability to apply one's knowledge to the solution of problems.

Cognition The primary way in which the teacher facilitates the accomplishment of these outcomes is through the appropriate use of the three goal structures discussed in this book. The heavy use of cooperation and the appropriate supplemental use of individualization and competition will do a great deal to ensure that the important cognitive outcomes discussed in Chapter 2 are achieved. But in order to determine the success of one's instructional program and to assess the competence and accomplishment of each student, the teacher must take certain periodic measures.

There are several ways in which the teacher collects information about student achievement of cognitive outcomes. The assignment of homework, papers, projects, problems, reports, and programmed units is one. The giving of quizzes, tests, and examinations is another. The observation of student behavior is a third. No attempt to review the first two procedures will be given here, as teachers generally receive a great deal of training in them. But some discussion of the use of observation procedures may be helpful.

You will have already gained some skill in observation through the procedures in Chapter 8. Now you can apply these skills not only to monitoring a goal structure but also to evaluating the outcomes of instruction. *Observation procedures* are aimed at describing and recording behavior as it occurs. From observing a student's behaviors, the teacher gains the information needed to make judgments about the current competence of the student and the success of the instructional program. Since you are the only person who can precisely pinpoint the desired instructional outcomes for your classes, you are also the appropriate person to design observation procedures. Seven steps to consider in designing these procedures are:

Research Design 1. *State your objectives in the appropriate behavioral form.* It is easy to describe outcomes in a general way; the tough job is to be more specific. For observational purposes, objectives must describe behavior that can be fairly easily seen and counted. In developing behavioral objectives keep in mind that you only have to be specific enough to observe pertinent behavior; it is possible to break mastering skills or knowledge into such small behaviors that there is no way to observe them all or that the pieces do not add up to the total skill. Keep in mind that it is not the specific behaviors that are important, it is the general outcomes that they represent. A form of "behavioral objective neurosis" results in losing sight of the forest in order to count the trees.

2. Construct an observation sheet. Your observation sheet should consist of a listing of the behaviors you want to observe, with space for noting their frequency.

3. Design a situation in which the desired behaviors can be displayed. This may be a testing situation or a summary assignment for students to work on.

4. Count the number of times each student engages in the desired behaviors. At this point you may wish to enlist the help of some of the students or of an aide if you're lucky enough to have one. If you are too busy conducting classes to spend much time observing, you can teach students to observe. Minimal training can make them quite proficient. If you are worried about this kind of use of student time, take a few minutes to chat with the students afterwards about what they learned in doing the observing. You will never want to turn it completely over to someone else. Plan some observing into your own schedule at intervals to check your counts against that of your other observers.

5. Examine the frequencies of student behaviors, and evaluate. In order to keep track of the information provided by observing, it is sometimes useful to use charts and graphs. Based upon the number of times students engaged in the specified behaviors, you judge whether or not your objectives have been accomplished (that is, whether students have mastered the desired skills, knowledge, concepts, principles, and procedures).

6. Be open to discovering unexpected and unplanned for outcomes. Any time you use a carefully worked out scheme of evaluation, it will be necessary to remind yourself to stay open to the unexpected. The unanticipated outcomes may be the most interesting and next time you cover the

◇◇◇

To practice the procedure on observing for accomplishment of cognitive objectives find a classroom and observe the problem-solving competencies. You can look for certain problem-solving skills such as defining a problem, diagnosing a problem's causes, specifying alternative solutions, deciding upon which solution to implement, implementing the solution, evaluating how well the solution worked. You can assign a series of problems to be solved, count the appropriate behaviors, evaluate, and look for unanticipated outcomes. After a few times, observation of students becomes automatic.

◇◇◇

same material, you may want to include them in your list of expected outcomes.

7. Record indirect class-related behaviors to supplement your observations. The number of students absent or late for class, the number of assignments completed on time, the number of optional assignments done, the number of students who ask questions about further work in an area, are all good indications of student mastery of cognitive objectives. Students can be used to organize such data for your use.

AFFECTIVE OUTCOMES

The affective outcomes of instruction are the attitudes and values students develop as a result of their experiences in school. There are long-term desired affective outcomes, such as developing democratic values and self-reliance, and short-term affective outcomes, such as enjoying a particular instructional unit. As discussed in Chapter 2, some of the important affective outcomes sought for by a school are gaining enjoyment and satisfaction from learning, appreciating of the various subject areas, valuing cultural, ethnic, and individual differences, valuing free and open inquiry into all problems, forming friendships with other students, helping, sharing, trusting, and caring while interacting with other students, and developing positive attitudes toward the school, the teachers and other school personnel, the instructional tasks, and education in general. Particularly important is the valuing of oneself and the appreciation of one's strengths, abilities, talents, and resources. In assessing these and other affective outcomes, it should be remembered that only the most important ones should be evaluated. If too many and too complex affective outcomes are measured, it will be difficult to obtain valid information, and it will be difficult to communicate the results of the evaluation. A small number of easily measured affective outcomes should be focused upon.

A teacher can assess affective outcomes of instruction through observation procedures or through questionnaires. The use of observation procedures has been discussed in the previous section. In preparing questionnaires, three types of questions can be used: semantic differential questions, open-ended questions, and closed-ended questions. The most general method for the measurement of attitudes is the semantic differential (Osgood et al., 1957). This type of question allows the teacher to present any attitude object (be it a person, issue, practice, musical composition, or anything else) and obtain an indication of the students' attitudes toward the object. A semantic differential question consists of a series of rating scales of bipolar adjective pairs underneath the concept the teacher wishes to obtain student attitudes toward. An example is:

Poetry

Beautiful	1 : 2 : 3 : 4 : 5 : 6 : 7	Ugly
Good	1 : 2 : 3 : 4 : 5 : 6 : 7	Bad
Fair	1 : 2 : 3 : 4 : 5 : 6 : 7	Unfair
Valuable	1 : 2 : 3 : 4 : 5 : 6 : 7	Worthless
Pleasant	1 : 2 : 3 : 4 : 5 : 6 : 7	Unpleasant

The teacher then sums the responses to obtain an overall indication of attitude towards the concept; using five 7-point scales the teacher could obtain scores that range from 5 to 35. Almost any concept of interest can be used in this type of question. An English teacher, for example, might want to explore attitudes toward drama, grammar, poetry, essay writing, English teachers, English class, or a specific writer, play, or poem. Each concept is repeated separately with the same set of adjectives. If a teacher does not use adjective pairs that are generally evaluative, such as those given above, she or he may wish to score the responses to each adjective pair sparately instead of summing them.

An open-ended question calls for the student to answer by writing a statement, which may vary in length. Examples of open-ended questions are:

My general opinion about _____ is . . .

If someone suggested you take up _____ as your life's work, what would you reply?

If you were asked to give a short talk about _____, what would you say?

My _____ teachers are . . .

What would you reply if one of your friends said, "_____ is very, very important, and everybody should try to learn as much about it as possible"?

My advice to other students considering taking _____ is . . .

Such open-ended questions will provide the teacher with interesting samples of student attitudes. Often you will find creative answers that may be helpful in deciding whether or not the affective objectives of the instructional program are being accomplished.

A closed-ended question requires the student to indicate the alternative answer that is closest to his internal response. Some samples are:

Do you intend to take another course in _____?

_____Yes _____No _____I'm not sure

How interested are you in learning more about _____?

Very interested 1 : 2 : 3 : 4 : 5 : 6 : 7 Very uninterested

If I had it to do over again, I (would/would not) have taken this subject.

I would like to teach English _____ than I would like to teach mathematics.

    a. A lot more
    b. A little more
    c. A little less
    d. A lot less

In comparison with other classes I have had, this class is:
    Superior 1 : 2 : 3 : 4 : 5 : 6 : 7   Inferior

Circle each of the words that tell how you feel about the subject of _____ .

interesting	very important	worthless
dull	useful	great
fun	useless	weird
difficult	boring	square
exciting	too easy	valuable

T   F   _____ is my favorite subject in school.

There are many different types of closed-ended questions; the ones listed above are only a few general examples. A teacher may wish to use other types of closed-ended questions he or she is familiar with.

A suggested procedure for using observations and questionnaires to measure the affective reactions of students to an instructional program is as follows:

1. Give your questionnaire, or make your observations, near the beginning and then near the end of a class unit or of an entire semester. From such a spacing, you will be able to calculate whether attitudes have improved or deteriorated as a result of the instructional program. If you use the same questions or observation categories for a few years, you will be able to build norms as to how most classes respond; such information is very helpful in determining the attitudes of a present class. In other words, *save your data.*

2. Since the measurement procedures suggested are rather crude, it is best to use more than one question to measure students' attitudes toward any one thing. It is advisable to use different types of questions dealing with the same topic. A combination of observations and questionnaire is often helpful. With a little practice you'll find that you can become a very good data gatherer.

3. Sharing the results with the class will indicate that their cooperation is appreciated and that the information is being used, and it will increase their motivation to give you valid data about how they respond to an instructional unit. It is important to make clear, however, that you are asking for feedback, not asking them to vote on class procedures.

Evaluating the Success of Goal Structures Flow Chart

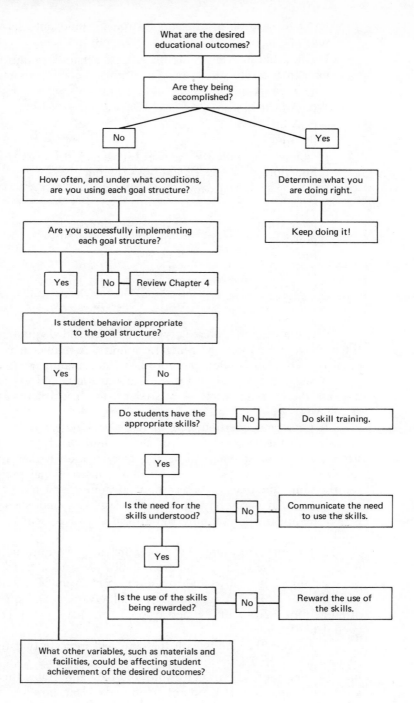

4. To increase the likelihood of getting honest responses, protect anonymity—do not ask students to put their names on the questionnaires; if a system of identification is desired, use one that keeps you from knowing which students responded in which ways. You might, for example, have each student make up a number combination and put it on all questionnaires measuring attitudes and values. If trust is high, however, names can be used.

5. Emphasize that you are asking students to indicate their attitudes and values in order to improve instruction and not to evaluate students. Make it clear that students will not be evaluated on the basis of their attitudes and values. Ask for student cooperation in giving honest reactions to instructional units and to their experience in the class and the school.

◇◇

Do not forget eavesdropping (the strategy described in Chapter 8). Although the information collected by eavesdropping is not quantitative like the information gathered through the observation and questionnaire procedures described in this chapter, it can be just as useful and interesting. It is certainly more personal in finding out what is going on in the learning situation. Review the procedures for evaesdropping and apply them to evaluating cognitive and affective outcomes.

◇◇

OVERALL SUMMARY OF STUDENT EVALUATION

In evaluating a single student you must do two things. First, you must collect and store information on each student. It is very helpful to express quantitatively all information collected about each student (in frequencies, percentages, points, and so on) because quantitative information allows great flexibility in summarizing or combining information from different sources and activities. Information collection is a crucial step in student evaluation because information is what you will base your value judgments on. You probably already have a storage system available, such as a folder for each student or a grade book.

Second, you must judge the information collected. The two major types of judgments you can make are *categorical judgments* and *comparative judgments.* *Categorical judgments* are made when you adopt a fixed set of standards and judge the achievement of each student against these standards. You use categorical judgments in evaluating student behavior in cooperative and individualistic situations. The *comparative judgments* are made when you compare the performance of one student with the performance of the other students to be judged; such comparative judgments are often called normative evaluation. Comparative judgments are used in interpersonal and intergroup competition situations.

◇◇

You are also making comparative judgments when you compare two performances of the same student (growth or change comparisons) and when you compare the actual performance of a student with the performance expected on the basis of his aptitude or ability (achievement comparisons). These comparative procedures are rarely used because of the difficulties in measuring change and in knowing what level of achievement to expect from a student.

◇◇

We can now discuss how a student is evaluated in each type of goal structure. In a *cooperative goal structure* each student will be working in a group to solve a problem or to complete a complex learning task. Within a cooperative situation each student will receive the score of her group. Thus if the group product is given a score of 90, each student will have 90 recorded in her performance record. When using a cooperative goal structure it will be necessary to make a categorical judgment about the group's performance (unless intergroup competition is being used, in which case a comparative judgment may be made). You will need to set up a standard as to how many points a group will receive for solving the assigned problem at different levels of proficiency.

In an *individualistic goal structure* each student will be working by herself to master the assigned factual material or skill. Each student receives points independently of other students. In such a situation a categorical judgment needs to be made; the teacher will set up a standard as to how many points a person will receive for mastering the assigned factual material or skill at different levels of proficiency and will give each student the appropriate number of points.

In a *competitive goal structure* comparative judgment is used. Each student receives points on the basis of how his performance compares with the performance of other students receiving the same instruction or working on the same task. The traditional grading on a "curve" is an example of this method.

Each student will participate in a variety of cooperative, individualistic, and competitive learning situations over a period of time within the classroom. When you wish to summarize the student's performance (say, at the end of every six weeks) the number of points the student receives is added up and the student's behavior is summarized. *At this point it is important that a categorical system be used if the student is to receive a specific single grade;* a comparative system in which the total number of points each student has is compared with the total number of points of other students would undermine all cooperative and individualistic learning situations in the future.

In most cases, in order to communicate effectively with students, parents, and other school personnel, you will wish to use a multi-dimensional summary of the student's performance. A summary sheet for such a purpose is shown on page 168. This summary sheet can be used in two ways. When specifically focusing upon an individual student the student's points should be placed in the table and the appropriate ratings made. When specifically focusing upon evaluating the instructional program, summarize the scores of all the students in some form, such as a group mean or average. The table has space for recording the total number of points the student(s) received and for a rating based on the total. Five ratings can be used: excellent, good, satisfactory, unsatisfactory, unacceptable.

Following is a list of the procedures needed to summarize your information about a student or an instructional program and to communicate your evaluation effectively.

1. Collect and store information on each student.
2. For cooperative and individualized sessions set your criteria for making categorical judgments about student performance. Seek help from the curriculum coordinator, subject matter specialists, teacher committees, the school administration and also from parents and students in setting your criteria.
3. For competitive sessions rank the students from best to worst.
4. Standardize your scoring system. Each student will participate in a variety of cooperative, individualized, and competitive learning situations over a period of time within your classroom. Students will need to understand your scoring system and how points are totaled in the evaluation process. Without a standardized system they will not be able to understand the evaluations.
5. Personalize your evaluation by including notes on incidents and behaviors, with dates, summaries of conferences with parents and other teachers, and long-term growth information. Actually this is the material most persons will be interested in. Using the eavesdropping procedures discussed in Chapter 8 is a good way of collecting information to bring your quantitative conclusions about a student's competence alive. Parents, other teachers, administrators, and even the student can relate more to actual episodes than to a summary number.

Summary Table

Student's Name ———————————————— Date ——————

Teacher's Name ———————————————— Class ——————

Cognitive Outcomes	*Points*	*Rating*
Mastery of factual material (Assignments, reports, quizzes, homework, work units)		
Mastery of assigned skills (work units, use in problem-solving situations, homework, reports)		
Mastery of concepts and principles (group scores, reports, homework, observations)		
Verbal ability 1. Communicates ideas and feelings effectively (observations, direct discussions with)		
2. Participates actively in problem-solving groups		
Writing ability (homework, reports)		
Cooperative ability (observations, group products)		
Competitive ability (observations, performances in competitions)		
Ability to work independently (observations, performances in individualized activities)		
Ability to apply knowledge and resources to the solution of problems (observations, group products)		

Affective Outcomes	*Points*	*Rating*
Has appreciation of subject area		
Appreciates learning (receives enjoyment and satisfaction from learning)		
Aware of, and appreciates, own abilities, achievements, talents, and resources		
When appropriate, helps others, shares resources, expresses warmth & caring, trusts		
Accepts and appreciates cultural, ethnic, and individual differences		
Willing to meet the expectations of others when it is appropriate		
Values free and open inquiry into all problems		

◇◇

Your objectives as a teacher are to encourage students to work toward accomplishing instructional goals with enthusiasm and optimism, to help each other achieve important goals, to compete with enjoyment for less important subgoals, to develop their individual competencies, and so on. Inappropriate competition prevents the accomplishment of such objectives. In summarizing student evaluations, therefore, if there is a danger that students or parents will make competitive comparisons, you may wish to stay away from a total summarizing score or, better yet, launch a campaign to educate students and parents to the purposes and goals of your evaluation.

◇◇

COMMUNICATING RESULTS

Once you have completed an evaluation of a student, what do you do next? An evaluation is useful only if it is communicated effectively to the appropriate audience. Successful communication depends upon the following:

1. *A set of symbols that has the same meaning for those who receive the message and for those who send the message.* If a teacher and a student's parents attach different meanings to the word "satisfactory," there will be little communication between them when the teacher uses "satisfactory" to describe the student's competencies. Some time must be spent in establishing a common language between the teacher and the audience so that evaluation words and symbols are interpreted in approximately the same way.

2. *Presentation of specific information about the teacher's frame of reference, criteria for different levels of student performance, procedures for gathering information, and instructional program.* In other words, a context for the evaluation has to be presented along with the results of the evaluation. This context is necessary to interpret the evaluation correctly.

3. *Repetition—for instance, present the evaluation both in written form and in a face-to-face discussion.* Such duplication is very helpful in ensuring effective communication.

4. *Opportunity for the audience to express what they understand the evaluation to mean.*

The most important communication of a student's evaluation is to the student. The results of an evaluation serve as direct information concerning the student's progress toward educational goals. The feedback that compares the actual performance of the student with the standard of performance desired increases the motivation of the student to learn and perform at a higher level. Such information should be immediate and explicit as possible. There is evidence that desired behaviors can often be

169

increased simply by being recorded and attended to (Broden, Hall, and Mitts, 1971). Thus evaluations will often motivate students to increase their achievement. Sitting down with a student and reviewing her progress and current performances is helpful to both the student and you (the teacher), especially when the student has a chance to react to the information being presented.

◇◇

Regardless of the particular form of evaluation and reporting, its success will depend primarily on the care that is taken in defining the system and the consistency with which that system is used.

◇◇

Communicating evaluations to parents, students, and other school personnel has often been an unpleasant task for teachers because of the competitive way in which the information was collected and evaluated. Telling parents that their child is not as competent as most other students in the class is not an easy task. But when all three goal structures have been appropriately used and when an evaluation plan that combines categorical and comparative evaluation has been used, communication with parents, students, and school personnel about a student's performance can focus on the student's strengths, abilities, needs, growth areas, talents, and potential. In addition, the contrasting of performance in the three goal structures can more precisely pinpoint problems students may have (as well as strengths) and result in constructive planning about how student performance can be improved in the future. It may be going too far to say that communicating evaluations will become enjoyable, but the job will surely improve markedly when you follow the procedures outlined in this book!

GRADES

No chapter on evaluation would be complete without some word about grades. Probably the most common way of communicating student evaluations is through grades. What are grades? *Grades* are an arbitrarily selected set of symbols employed to transmit information from teachers to students, parents, and school personnel. A single-mark system has received a great deal of criticism on the grounds that a single mark cannot possibly give a full picture of the many different facets of achievement and that a single mark is limited to one particular frame of reference. Persons often overgeneralize grades so that they are taken as an indication of a student's total competence and worth as an individual. Many schools, therefore, have adopted a multiple marking system as an alternative to the traditional single-mark approach.

"a threefold cord is not quickly broken"

Eccles. 4:13

TEN

teacher concerns
and classroom management
last-minute advice

INTRODUCTION

In this book the authors have tried to build a bridge between the social psychological knowledge of goal structures and the practices of teachers in real classrooms with real students. The first part of the book builds a foundation for teacher effectiveness by presenting the rationale for using goal structures. The rest of the book spells out how to put that knowledge into practice. The theory of goal structures becomes a teaching process of goal structuring, monitoring, and evaluating. The next step is for you, the reader, to extend the ideas in this book to your situation, modify them where it is needed to fit your classroom, and put them into practice. The reward for doing so is that teaching will be more enjoyable, more productive, and easier.

In our work with teachers to put these ideas to use in their classrooms, several teacher concerns have been continually expressed. This chapter presents some of these concerns and our joint attempts to solve them from what we have learned. Perhaps you will have some of these concerns as you implement the material in this book in your teaching. If so, you should find this final information helpful.

CLASSROOM MANAGEMENT

The major concerns of many teachers are classroom management, classroom control, and classroom discipline. Teachers are continually told by administrators, colleagues, parents, teacher educators, and the man-on-the-street in subtle and not so subtle ways that classroom control is the most important part of teaching. It isn't! Certainly, any time you have twenty-five to forty people together in a room there are going to be some coordination and organizing problems to be solved. Managing the classroom is just an initial step toward the more important goals that relate to cognitive and affective learning. The cause of most discipline problems is the inappropriate use of competitive and individualized goal structures and the underuse of the cooperative goal structure. *The skillful use of the three goal structures will reduce the causes of discipline problems and ensure that they are not compounded through further aggravation!* Is it hard to believe this statement? We believe we can safely make it. Consider the effects of the appropriate use of cooperation on (1) disruptive, nonresponsive, unmotivated students, (2) depressed, shy, isolated, disliked students, and (3) student-student conflict.

Within most traditional classrooms there are students who are resistant to teacher influence, unmotivated to learn what is being taught, nonresponsive to the usual rewards teachers have to offer for appropriate behavior, and inappropriately aggressive, hostile, obstructive, irritating, and disobedient. Controlling and disciplining these students is a major problem for most teachers. Yet the results of research on cooperation show a way to minimize such problems! *The appropriate use of cooperation will reduce inappropriate, nonresponsive, and obstructive behavior on the part of students!* In a cooperative situation students work together to achieve mutual goals and, therefore, are susceptible to influence from each other. There is considerable research that demonstrates that cooperators do exert influence on and accept influence from each other (see Appendix A). This mutual influence results in more peer encouragement for achievement and a climate more oriented toward academic involvement. Instead of approval and support for learning coming from the teacher, it comes from peers. Instead of a student's demonstrating independence from adults by disobeying the teacher a student demonstrates concern for his peers by helping the group achieve. A student who couldn't care less what grade the teacher assigns his work will care a great deal about how his peers view the quality of his effort. Hostility toward authority will not be expressed when working cooperatively with one's peers. Unmotivated, nonresponsive, obstructive students can be substantially helped by placing them in cooperative relationships in which there will be positive peer influences. The effectiveness of communication among cooperators, the level of trust built in cooperative groups, the peer-tutoring that is available in cooperative learning situations, the student preference for, involvement in, and liking of cooperative experiences—all will contribute to positive peer influence in cooperative situations. Even if you had time to work individually with every student, you could not have as much influence on the student's behavior as do the student's peers. Cooperative groupings will reduce your discipline problems and the cooperative situation is far different from the one in which you are expected to motivate, counsel, and discipline every student you come into contact with. (If you are worried about the way students exert influence on each other review the discussion of cooperative myths in Chapter 3).

Most traditional classrooms have students who are isolated because of their shyness, depression, or negative self-attitudes, or because for one reason or another students have taken a disliking to them. Teachers are often at a loss as to how to help such students, how to integrate them more fully into classroom life. The research on cooperation provides an answer (see Appendix A). *The appropriate use of cooperation will reduce isolation of shy, depressed, disliked, fearful students.* Cooperation requires interaction among students, thus reducing the isolation of all. Cooperative interaction results in positive interpersonal relationships characterized by mutual liking, positive attitudes toward each other, mutual concern, friendliness, and attentiveness; it also promotes positive self-attitudes and success experiences, which come about from contributing to group efforts and the utilization of one's resources by the group. As will be discussed below, even when students dislike each other intensely, view each other in negative ways, or want to avoid contact with each other, cooperation in achieving several mutually desired goals produces mutual liking and appreciation. You may help reduce isolation (and student shyness, depression, fear of rejection, and negative self-attitudes) when you encourage cooperation among students.

A major problem for teachers is the mediating role they are required to play in conflicts among students. Student-student conflicts can cause innumerable headaches for teachers. Teachers are rarely given specific training in conflict management or in the procedures for resolving conflicts. *The appropriate use of goal structures, however, will reduce conflict among students and promote constructive management of the conflicts that do arise.* There are two basic principles for you to remember in dealing with student-student conflicts: (1) the overuse and inappropriate use of competition produces conflicts among students, and (2) cooperative experiences reduce conflict among students. There is considerable research support for these statements (see Appendix A). Thus teachers who have students who are regularly in conflict (and who doesn't?) may reduce the likelihood of future conflict by having the students cooperate on a series of projects and avoiding inappropriate competition.

Of special interest to schools and classroom teachers is the problem of reducing student prejudice toward groups and individuals who are in some way different from the middle-class white majority. Ethnic groups, the lower socioeconomic groups, physically and mentally handicapped persons, and even the aged, are discriminated against because of their "difference." Such prejudices create a great deal of student-student conflict in heterogeneous schools. Many teachers throughout the United States are required to mediate student-student conflicts based upon ethnic and cultural differences. *The appropriate use of cooperation among students can reduce substantially the amount of interethnic and intercultural conflict in the classroom and the school.* There is considerable research that demonstrates that such conflict will disappear after several weeks of cooperation among students from different backgrounds (see Appendix A). Students in a cooperative relationship are, in general, accepting of each other. Since a heterogeneous group will problem solve better than a homogeneous group, differences among students become appreciated, valued, and utilized for goal accomplishment. In a cooperative setting, students learn to value differences, as they are useful in a division of labor and in problem solving and facilitate the productivity of the group.

RETURN TO THE MYTH OF THE LAZY STUDENT

Many teachers we have worked with are concerned with the "lazy" student in a cooperating group who lets the others do all the work but shares in the benefits. As discussed in Chapter 3, the "lazy" student is one of the myths about cooperative groups. With cooperation comes increased commitment and involvement that eliminates the possibility of parasites. Yet, if you have an occasional unmotivated student in your classroom, here are some things you may try. First, you may ask the group to discuss the issue with the student and see why he is not contributing his share to the group's work. The group may be able to find a way to facilitate increased contributions by the student. Second, you may take the student aside and ask about the situation, seeking to determine his perception of the situation and what he thinks he can do about it. Problem solving the alternative ways in which more commitment or involvement can be obtained is always a helpful process. Third, you can relax and let the group deal with the student in its own way and in its own time. This is often a very valuable learning experience for all students involved, and being too quick to intervene in such situations can seriously interfere with the education of your students.

Fourth, you can present a skills lesson on problem solving such a situation in order to be sure that the students have the skills they need to deal with the "lazy" student constructively.

An unobtrusive way of highlighting the situation is to change the method by which the group score is calculated. One effective method that several researchers have used is to average the scores of the lowest members of the group. When all students are doing the same thing (such as completing a set of math problems), such a procedure can be used. It will motivate the group members to tutor the poorer students in the group, thereby resolving any problems with commitment and involvement in the learning tasks.

INDIVIDUALIZED INSTRUCTION AND STUDENT INTERACTION

Many teachers ask the authors why it is not possible to individualize instruction and still have students interacting and helping each other. Like many key words in education, individualize is being stretched to include so many different practices that it is growing less and less useful as a descriptor. Critics of education often state that teachers never change their behavior, they just change the words describing their behavior. The original intent of individualizing instruction was to help a student develop individual goals so that he might work toward goal accomplishment in his own way and at his own pace, in a manner and sequence suited to him personally. Such a procedure (while useful in promoting mastery of facts and noncomplex skills) is not intended to encourage student-student interaction. Requests by students for help from other students disrupt and interrupt goal accomplishment in an individualistic goal structure. It is also difficult for a student to be of assistance when his style of working is much different from that of another student, and when both are working on different, individualized goals. If you want to have students helping each other, interacting in positive ways, and sharing materials and resources, it is better to move to a cooperative goal structure rather than trying to stretch individualizing to cover all learning situations. If you are concerned about this issue, it may be helpful to review the discussions on when to use individualized goal structures in Chapter 4 and the myths about individualizing in Chapter 3.

COMPETITION AND MOTIVATION

Inappropriate competition does not increase motivation—it kills it. This point was discussed in the section on competitive myths in Chapter 3. Yet many teachers remain unconvinced. Perhaps the most powerful statement on the subject was made by John Atkinson, the foremost psychologist in the area of achievement motivation (Atkinson and Raynor, 1974, page xi):

Achievement is a we thing, not a me thing, always the product of many heads and hands no matter how it may appear to one involved in the effort and enjoyment of it or to a casual observer.

Motivation to achieve is not based upon competition with others but upon believing that there is a reasonable chance to accomplish a desired goal. The research clearly demonstrates that cooperation is much more facilitative of motivated effort and achievement than is competition (see Appendix A). There is nothing else that can be said on this issue.

STUDENTS WHO MUST ALWAYS WIN

What can be done with "life or death" competitors who approach all competition with taut muscles and high anxiety and miss the enjoyment and fun in the situation? Some students become so concerned with always winning (or never losing) that they can't learn to compete for fun and to enjoy the situation, win or lose. Especially when such competitive attitudes carry over to individualistic and cooperative situations, the inappropriate behaviors of the student are evident.* Some suggestions for helping such a student are as follow:

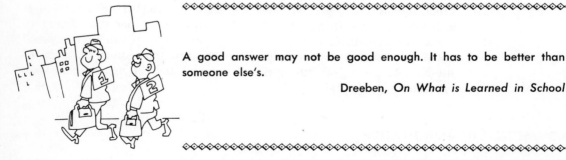

A good answer may not be good enough. It has to be better than someone else's.

Dreeben, *On What is Learned in School*

* For several years, the two authors competed inappropriately at Christmas by trying to determine who got the most presents. This not only ruined Christmas for the two of us but gave the rest of the family headaches. The behavior stopped when the rest of the family started giving the two authors aches in certain places whenever such a competition began!

First, find a good model in another student and put him in some low-key, friendly competitive situations with the overcompetitive student. Then reward fun and involvement rather than winning, while pointing out that taking competition too seriously takes the enjoyment out of it. A second approach is to reinforce cooperation whenever the overcompetitive student engages in it. A third possible approach is to ask the student to build a plan for reducing his competitiveness; you may provide any counseling she needs for constructing and implementing such a plan.

◇◇

Math Tournament

One teacher constructed a math tournament among students in the following manner. Students were divided into clusters of four students. A series of weekly quiz questions was placed in a jar in the center of the table. The first student would draw a question from the jar and try to solve it. The other three students would then evaluate his answer and determine whether it was right or wrong. The second student would then draw a question from the jar, and so on, until all the quiz questions had been answered. The winner was the student who had answered the most questions correctly, and the other students were ranked second, third, and last. Winners across groups were compared to see who had the best performance in the class. This same procedure can be used in any type class.

◇◇

APPROPRIATENESS OF A GOAL STRUCTURE FOR A STUDENT

Many teachers have asked us whether certain students wouldn't do better if the teacher always used the same goal structure with them rather than varying goal structures according to desired outcomes of instruction. Certain students may have a predisposition and preference to compete, cooperate, or work individually. Yet a person who is going to function effectively in society must have the skills to do all three. It is not a question of matching the goal structure and the student; it is a question of the responsibility of the school (this means the teacher) to socialize students into the skills they need in order to be productive members of society.

GOAL STRUCTURES AND YOUR CLASSROOM

"Your ideas on goal structures sound good for _____ (insert your favorite target), but they won't work in my classroom (insert a description of your classroom)!" We have heard this statement often in the past four years. If you are doubtful that the ideas in this book can really be used in your classroom, stop and consider again. The research reviewed in Appendix A was conducted with all age groups in a variety of situations, from marble rolling to university-level examinations in psychology. *The material in this book is appropriate for any teaching situation,* whether it is a preschool program or a graduate school, whether it is a mathematics or a social studies class, whether it is vocational education or liberal arts. Any teacher who wishes to promote higher achievement, more positive attitudes, and broader educational outcomes, should consider goal structuring as part of her instructional program.

In this book we have emphasized that cooperation should be used primarily with problem-solving activities. In many classrooms the majority of time is spent on basic skills, which some teachers assume cannot be taught in cooperative ways. Yet several research studies demonstrate clearly that performance (for all group members) on math problems is higher in a cooperative group than when students work individualistically or in competition with each other. Math and other basic skills involve learning concepts that are best done under cooperative conditions. Thus, even if you teach basic skills, you will want to use all three goal structures appropriately.

THE HUMANIZATION OF STUDENTS

Students learn how to be human through interpersonal relationships in which people communicate honestly and openly, sharing themselves with each other. As has been constantly referred to in this book, how students interact depends upon the goal structure being used by the teacher. The goal structure promotes a pattern of interaction (which determines the learning climate), which in turn promotes certain cognitive and affective outcomes of instruction. While the individual student is regarded as the focus of the learning process, it must be remembered that a person's psychological experiences and behavior are based upon interpersonal relationships and are influenced strongly by group norms. The interpersonal relationships formed in the classroom are highly important for learning. If the classroom is characterized only by superficial and distant relationships, covert hostility and cynicism, and little mutual concern or respect among students and between the teacher and the students, little learning will take place. Students and teachers cannot learn and work within a hostile and alienating environment. Positive and significant relationships must be formed among members of the classroom. The only effective way to promote the development of such relationships is through the appropriate use of the three goal structures and especially through the frequent use of cooperation. *The application of the material in this book will do more to humanize students and the school than any other possible teacher behavior.*

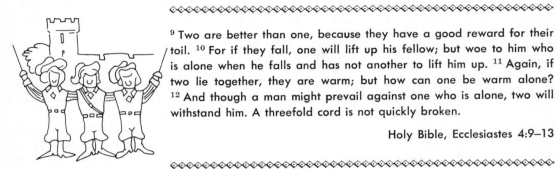

◇◇

[9] Two are better than one, because they have a good reward for their toil. [10] For if they fall, one will lift up his fellow; but woe to him who is alone when he falls and has not another to lift him up. [11] Again, if two lie together, they are warm; but how can one be warm alone? [12] And though a man might prevail against one who is alone, two will withstand him. A threefold cord is not quickly broken.

Holy Bible, Ecclesiastes 4:9–13

◇◇

COOPERATION AMONG TEACHERS

Cooperation among students will be easier to establish and maintain if there is cooperation among school personnel. Many schools are scarred by competition among teachers. In these schools, teachers feel insecure, isolated, cold, reserved, defensive, and competitive in their relationships with their fellow teachers and the administrators. Feelings of hostility, guardedness, and alienation toward the rest of the school staff create anxiety in teachers, which in turn decreases their effectiveness in the classroom. The teachers act as though they never need help from their colleagues. A fiction is maintained that a "professional and highly trained teacher" has already achieved sufficient competence and skill to handle alone all classroom situations. The actual result, however, is that innovative and creative teaching is stifled by insecurity, anxiety, and competitiveness. And the environment is depressing and discouraging.

One of the most constructive contributions you can make to your school is to encourage cooperation among teachers and the use of the cooperative goal structure in the classroom. How do you encourage teacher cooperation? The process is the same as implementing cooperation among students. Establish cooperative goals that all involved teachers wish to accomplish and that require interdependence and interaction among the teachers. Sufficient trust and openness must be present for teachers to feel free to visit one another's classrooms and ask one another for help or suggestions. Providing feedback about each other's teaching and providing help to increase teaching skills are equally important. Teachers must have the basic communication, trust building, and controversy skills discussed in Chapter 6. Team teaching, coordinating all social studies curricula, establishing support groups in which teachers provide help and assistance to each other, coordinating the teaching of difficult students, all are examples of cooperative interaction among teachers. However you do it, implementing department- and school-wide cooperation among teachers will immensely increase your enjoyment of teaching and of working in your school, and it will encourage cooperation among students within your classroom.

CONCLUSION

There are without a doubt more teacher concerns than those we have discussed in this chapter and after mastering the material in this book, you may be just as able to discuss the concerns of teachers and provide answers to them as we are. You may at this point wish to review the section on teaching effectiveness in Chapter 1. How would you rate your teaching effectiveness now? How would you rate your ability to use successfully and appropriately the cooperative, competitive, and individualized goal structures? Through continued use of the three goal structures, you will improve your teaching, make it more enjoyable, and make teaching easier for yourself. If you won't take our word for that, try it and see for yourself!

epilogue

In retrospect, a couple of points need to be stressed. Although we have discussed thoroughly all three goal structures, cooperation is what this book is about. It is the context in which both competition for fun and individualistically working on one's own take place. Cooperation gives meaning to the knowledge and skills gained in the other two goal structures, as it is within cooperative activities that such knowledge and skills are used to create alternatives and solve problems. This is as true of society as a whole as it is of instruction in schools. Cooperation is the "air" of society, which we constantly breathe, completely necessary to us, but relatively unnoticed. We do notice changes in the air, a whiff of perfume or a blanket of smog, but these are the rare instances. Like the perfume, the times we are locked (or licked) in competition and the things we achieve "on our own" stand out and are remembered because they are different from the majority of our efforts, which are cooperative. Just as the parochial myth that "smog is what most air is like and we need to learn to live with it" can grow in the minds of those who live in a large city so egocentric myths like "it's a survival of the fittest society" have grown and have been nourished by those who ignore the many cooperative aspects of their lives while concentrating on those aspects that are perceived as competitive. In our society (and school) we share a common language, we drive on the appropriate side of the street, we take turns going out doors, we raise families, we seek friendship, we share the maintenance of life through an intricate division of labor. This is not to say that the skills of competition and individualization are unimportant. They are important, but only within the larger context of cooperation with others, and a person needs to know when to compete or work individualistically and when to cooperate. Unfortunately, instruction in schools at present seems to stress competition or perhaps individualization without much attention to the skills needed to facilitate effective cooperation. To encourage a positive and effective learning environment, to promote the achievement and socialization outcomes of schools, we must realize that cooperation is the forest—competition and individualization are but trees.

As the authors look back on the aspects of our growing up together that we shared with the reader in the preface and in various parts of this book, we realize that we may have misled you. The competition between us was a rather small part of the time we spent together. What made the instances of competition bearable was the constant supportive cooperation within our family, and later with our friends and our own families.

Without cooperation and the skills that it requires, life in a society or a school would be impossible.

APPENDIX A
review of research

In order to minimize the references included in the text of this book, the authors have chosen to place a review of research as an appendix. The following is the research upon which the theory presented in this book is based.

COGNITIVE PREREQUISITES

Certain cognitive prerequisites are necessary for a person to respond appropriately to a cooperative, competitive, or individualistic goal structure. First, one has to be aware of the existence of other individuals; second, he has to be able to identify and respond to their actions, and third, he must be aware of the nature of the goal interdependence and to understand what implications the goal structure has for one's own and the others' behavior. A person must realize that the outcomes of the situation depend upon the

behavior of oneself and other individuals; in other words, there is an awareness of mutual causation in the situation. Within a cooperative goal structure, such understanding will be reflected in mutual assistance; within a
competitive situation such understanding will be reflected in attempts to
obstruct others' goal accomplishments, and in individualistic goal structures
such understanding will be reflected in ignoring others' behavior. The research by Madsen and his students indicates that the ability to comprehend
interdependency develops after the age of five and before the age of ten
(Nelson and Kagan, 1972). Finally, a person must be able to take other
persons' perspectives in the sense of imagining what is in other persons'
minds and of forming hypotheses concerning what persons will do in response to the goal structure. A person must be able to recognize and take
into account the perspective and strategy of other individuals. This ability
will be discussed more fully in the section on outcomes.

TRADITONAL USE OF COMPETITION

Traditionally, an interpersonal competition goal structure in which students are expected to outperform their peers has been used in American
education. There is evidence that (1) most students perceive school as
being competitive (R. T. Johnson, D. W. Johnson, and Bryant, 1973; R. T.
Johnson, 1974; D. W. Johnson, 1973a), (2) American children are more
competitive than are children from other countries (Madsen and Shapira,
1970; Madsen, 1971; Kagan and Madsen, 1971, 1972; Nelson and Kagan,
1972), (3) American children become more competitive the longer they
are in school or the older they become (Nelson, 1970; Madsen, 1971; Madsen and Conner, 1973; Nelson and Kagan, 1972), (4) Anglo-American
children are more competitive than are other American children, for instance, Mexican-American and Afro-American children (Kagan and Madsen, 1971; Madsen and Shapira, 1970), and (5) urban children are more
competitive than are rural children (Madsen, 1967; Shapira and Madsen,
1969; Kagan and Madsen, 1971, 1972; Miller and Thomas, 1972; Nelson
and Kagan, 1972). In reviewing the research of Millard C. Madsen and his
students, Nelson and Kagan (1972) state that the tendency for children
to compete in conflict-of-interest situations often interfered with their
capacity for adaptive, cooperative problem solving. They found that American students so seldom cooperate spontaneously on the experimental tasks
that it appears that the environment provided for these children is barren
of experiences that would sensitize them to the possibility of cooperation.
Not only do American children engage in irrational and self-defeating competition but the Anglo-American child (in comparison with children from
other countries, for instance, Mexico) is willing to reduce his own reward
in order to reduce the reward of a peer. The socialization of American

children into competitive attitudes and orientations is so pervasive that Staub (1971) found that American children often believe that helping a person in distress is inappropriate and is disapproved of by others.

PROCESS VARIABLES

By learning processes, the authors are referring to the way in which students interact and behave in learning situations. Process variables are predominantly factors influencing the interpersonal and group behavior within the instructional situation. The research indicates that several process variables are affected by goal structures. Almost all the process variables mentioned (with the notable exception of anxiety) affect problem-solving behavior but not behavior in simple drill activities that require no help from other students. The specific findings of the research on goal structures is as follows.

The amount of anxiety experienced by students in an instructional situation has to be of major concern to educators. High levels of anxiety significantly interfere with learning (e.g., several students have demonstrated that individuals who experience high levels of anxiety suffer a loss in efficiency in processing information they receive and a loss in the ability to abstract and in other flexibilities of intellectual functioning), and a continual experience of even moderate levels of anxiety may result in psychological damage and even physiological harm. Although the relationship between anxiety and learning is more complex than the research on anxiety and goal structures has assumed (e.g., different types of anxiety and tasks need to be taken into account), several research studies have focused upon the amount of anxiety experienced by students in a cooperative or a competitive structure. It seems probable that higher levels of anxiety and a more continued state of anxiety would be found in competitive structures, as the risk of failing to accomplish a desired goal or to receive a desired reward may be higher; in addition, "losing" may result in a decrease in self-esteem or in esteem from other individuals, either of which may promote anxiety concerning one's performance.

Competition has been found to increase anxiety in students performing a motor-steadiness task (Naught and Newman, 1966). Haines and McKeachie (1967) found that students in a competitively structured discussion were more anxious, less self-assured, and showed more incidences of self-oriented needs; students in a cooperatively structured discussion were described as less tense and more task oriented. Deutsch (1949b) found evidence that students in cooperative groups were more secure than students in competitive groups. Blau (1954) found that adults working in a large industry were more anxious when working in a competitive structure than when working in a cooperative structure. There is some evidence that these findings hold true for younger children as well; Stendler, Damrin, and Haines (1951) studied seven-year-olds and found that destructive, boastful, and depreciatory behavior exceeded friendly conversation, sharing, and helping behavior when a task was structured competitively, while the reverse was true when the task was structured cooperatively. These studies suggest that cooperative goal structures produce less anxiety for students and provide a better learning climate, especially for students who are chronically anxious and tense, than do competitive goal structures. The friendlier, more supportive atmosphere within the cooperative goal structure would tend to reduce anxiety for the highly anxious student, making his task easier, while the more aggressive atmosphere fostered in the competitive goal structure would tend to increase or maintain anxiety in highly anxious students, making their learning tasks more difficult. In a discussion of anxiety generated by making errors in an open school, Rathborne (1970) notes that the teacher's attitude toward errors contributes to the overall psychological climate of the classroom; the fear of failure is not great when errors are treated as normal, nonreprehensible parts of the learning process. The establishment of a cooperative goal structure does facilitate a climate in which it is possible to benefit from mistakes as opposed to one in which mistakes must be hidden in order to avoid ridicule.

Positive interpersonal relations among students is necessary both for effective problem solving in groups and for general classroom enjoyment of instructional activity. The psychological safety and security necessary for open exploration of instructional tasks is based upon feelings of being accepted, liked, and supported by fellow students. Class cohesion is based upon positive interpersonal relationship among students. The research strongly supports the proposition that cooperative goal structures encourage positive interpersonal relationships characterized by mutual liking, positive attitudes toward each other, mutual concern, friendliness, attentiveness, feelings of obligation to other students, and desire to win the respect of other students (Anderson, 1939; Deutsch, 1949b; French, 1951; Stendler, Damrin, and Haines, 1951; Blau, 1954; Gottheil, 1955; Phillips and D'Amico, 1956; Wilson and Miller, 1961; Sherif et al., 1961; Myers, 1962; Raven and Eachus, 1963; Crombag, 1966; Krauss, 1966; McClintock and McNeel, 1967; Julian and Perry, 1967; Swingle and Coady, 1967; Haines and McKeachie, 1967; Uejio and Wrightsman, 1967; Cook, 1969, 1971; Wheeler, 1972; DeVries and Edwards, 1973, 1974; Ryan and Wheeler, 1973; Scott and Cherrington, 1974; Bryant and Crockenberg, 1974; DeVries, Edwards and Wells, 1974b; Bryant, Crockenberg and Wilce, 1974; Weigel, Wiser and Cook, 1974; Blanchard, Adelman, and Cook, 1974). The majority of these same studies demonstrate that competitive goal structures have a negative effect on interpersonal relations among students!

An explanation for these findings on interpersonal relations is that there is considerable evidence that we like those who facilitate our goal accomplishment (Deutsch, 1949b; Berkowitz and Daniels, 1963; Secord and Backman, 1964; Goranson and Berkowitz, 1966; Zajonc and Marin, 1967; Ashmore, 1970; D. W. Johnson and S. Johnson, 1972; S. Johnson and D. W. Johnson, 1972; Blanchard, Adelman, and Cook, 1974; Weigel, Wiser, and Cook, 1974; Blanchard, Weigel, and Cook, 1974;) and dislike those who frustrate our goal accomplishment (Deutsch, 1949b; Burnstein and Worchel, 1962; Zajonc and Marin, 1967; Ashmore, 1970; D. W. Johnson and S. Johnson, 1972; S. Johnson and D. W. Johnson, 1972; Blanchard, Adelman, and Cook, 1974; Weigel, Wiser, and Cook, 1974; Blanchard, Weigel, and Cook, 1974). To be in a cooperative goal structure with another person, therefore, produces positive relationships and to be in a competitive relationship with another person tends to produce negative relationships. Even when individuals dislike each other intensely or come from groups engaged in high levels of conflict, cooperation in achieving several mutually desired goals produces positive intergroup and interpersonal relationships (Sherif et al., 1961; Blake and Mouton, 1962; D. W. Johnson and Lewicki, 1969).

Low achievers, who pulled the performance of the group down, were not disliked by or alienated from their peers in cooperative situations (DeVries, Edwards, and Wells, 1974b).

Social isolates are more often integrated into classroom friendship circles under cooperative than under competitive conditions (DeVries and Mescon, 1974).

There is evidence that under cooperative goal structures communication among students will be open, effective, and accurate, whereas in competitive situations communication will be closed, ineffective, and inaccurate (Deutsch, 1949b, 1962; French, 1951; Grossack, 1954; Deutsch and Krauss, 1962; Krauss and Deutsch, 1966; Crombag, 1966; Fay, 1970; D. W. Johnson, 1971, 1973d; Bonoma, Tedeschi, and Helm, 1974). Blake and Mouton (1961) provide evidence that competition biases a person's perceptions and comprehension of viewpoints and positions of other individuals. In any instructional situation in which students are required to share ideas and engage in information exchange, competition will have destructive effects, while a cooperative goal structure will facilitate such activities.

Deutsch (1958, 1960, 1962) and other researchers have found that trust is built through cooperative interaction and destroyed through competitive interaction. Thus educators interested in building trusting climates facilitative of problem solving will use cooperative and avoid competitive goal structures.

There will be more mutual influence in cooperative than in competitive goal structures (Deutsch, 1949b; Raven and Eachus, 1963; Crombag,

1966). Mutual influence is vital for effective problem solving. Several studies have found the normative peer climate more oriented toward academic involvement and peer encouragement for achievement much stronger under cooperative goal structures than under competitive goal structures (Deutsch, 1949b; Spilerman, 1971; DeVries, Muse, and Wells, 1971; DeVries and Edwards, 1974; DeVries, Edwards, and Wells, 1974b; Hulten, 1974). The acceptance of peer influence toward increased achievement will facilitate instructional success. Haines and McKeachie (1967) found students more task oriented under cooperative conditions.

In order for effective learning and problem solving to take place, students need to share ideas and materials and help each other. There is evidence that more peer tutoring is found in cooperatively structured situations than in competitive or individualistic situations (Hamblin, Buckholdt, Ferritor, Kozloff, and Blackwell, 1971; Hamblin, Hathaway and Wodarski, 1971; Wodarski, Hamblin, Buckholdt, and Ferritor, 1971, 1972, 1973, 1974; Buckholdt, Ferritor, and Tucker, 1974; Witte, 1972; DeVries and Edwards, 1973, 1974; DeVries, Edwards and Wells, 1974b; DeVries and Mescon, 1974; Weigel, Wiser, and Cook, 1974). Deutsch (1949b) found more behavior directed toward helping the group improve its functioning under cooperative conditions than under competitive conditions. His overall findings demonstrate that students attempt to obstruct each other's success under competitive conditions.

There is consistent evidence that students will become more involved in instructional activities and tasks under cooperative than under competitive conditions (Deutsch, 1949b; Hammond and Goldman, 1961; Haines and McKeachie, 1967). Students in cooperative groups attached greater importance to achieving than did students in competition with each other (Hulten, 1974). There is evidence that students prefer and like cooperatively structured over competitively structured learning situations (DeVries and Edwards, 1973; R. T. Johnson, D. W. Johnson, and Bryant, 1973; D. W. Johnson, 1973a; Wheeler and Ryan, 1973; R. T. Johnson, 1974). It seems reasonable to assume that the degree to which one prefers the goal structure one is operating within will affect one's involvement in the situation and motivation to complete the assigned tasks.

There will be more coordination of efforts, subdivision of activity, and division of labor within cooperatively structured situations than in competitive or individualistic situations (Deutsch, 1949b; Mintz, 1951; Thomas, 1957).

In order to engage successfully in problem solving, there must be a period in which diversity of ideas and information are suggested and divergent thinking emphasized; the overall evidence indicates that this will be more likely to happen under a cooperative goal structure (Deutsch, 1949b; DeVries and Edwards, 1974). There is some evidence that individuals will take greater risks in their thinking and actions in a cooperatively structured situation (Kogan and Wallach, 1967).

Cooperative, as compared with individualistic and competitive, goal structures will promote studying behavior and decrease apathetic, non-studying, and disruptive behaviors on the part of students and talking on the part of teachers (Wodarski et al. 1973; DeVries, Edwards and Wells, 1974a).

COGNITIVE OUTCOMES

There is considerable research on the cognitive outcomes of cooperative, individualistic, and competitive goal structures. Most of this research has compared cooperative and competitive goal structures. It should be noted that much of the research comparing cooperative and competitive goal structures has actually compared the use of interpersonal competition with the use of a combination of intragroup cooperation and intergroup competition. Evidence by Edwards and DeVries (1974a) and DeVries, Edwards, and Wells (1974b) indicates that students in an intragroup cooperation, intergroup competition situation behave primarily as if the intergroup competition did not exist, thus indicating that the results of such studies are due to the cooperativeness of the situation.

The research indicates that competition may be superior to cooperative or individualistic goal structures when a task is a simple drill activity or when sheer quantity of work is desired on a mechanical or skill-oriented task that requires little if any help from another person (Triplett, 1897; Chapman and Feder, 1917; Hurlock, 1927; Maller, 1929; Phillips, 1954; Miller and Hamblin, 1963; Clayton, 1964; Julian and Perry, 1967; Clifford, 1971; Scott and Cherrington, 1974). Children, for example, pick up pegs or carry marbles more efficiently when the situation is structured competitively (Sorokin, Tranquist, Parten, and Zimmerman, 1930). When tasks become somewhat more complex, for instance, solving math problems or recalling significant dates and names, cooperation results in higher achievement than does competition (Edwards, DeVries, and Snyder, 1972; Edwards and DeVries, 1974; DeVries, Edwards, and Wells, 1974a; Hulten, 1974).

When the task is some sort of problem-solving activity, the research clearly indicates that a cooperative goal structure results in higher achievement than does a competitive goal structure (Almack, 1930; Husband, 1940; Krugman, 1944; Deutsch, 1949b; Shaw, 1958; Jones and Vroom, 1964; O'Connell, 1965; Laughlin and McGlynn, 1967; Gurnee, 1968; Baker, 1968; DeVries and Mescon, 1974; Okun and DiVesta, 1974). A number of studies demonstrate that cooperative goal structures are more effective than are competitive goal structures in increasing group productivity (French, 1951; Smith, Madden, and Sobol, 1957; Thomas, 1957; Shaw, 1958; Willis and Joseph, 1959; Hammond and Goldman, 1961; Raven and Eachus, 1963; Crombag, 1966). Memorization and the retrieval of information from one's memory is often required in classroom learning, and there is evidence that cooperative group discussions are superior to competitive group discussions in facilitating individual memory of what was discussed (Yuker, 1955; Smith, Madden and Sobol, 1957) and that more analysis and memorization level activities take place in cooperative (compared to competitive) goal structures (DeVries, Edwards, and Wells, 1974a). If the instructional task requires students to be dependent upon each other, competitive motivation will interfere with problem solving (Miller and Hamblin, 1963; Nelson and Kagan, 1972). Low achieving students are especially benefited by cooperatively structured learning activities (DeVries and Mescon, 1974).

Fay (1970) found that fifth and sixth grade girls learned a great deal more when they were members of cooperative groups than when they belonged to competitive groups. A series of other studies, however, have found that while daily performance is superior under a cooperative goal structure there are no significant differences on examination performance among individuals who studied in a competitive or cooperative group (Deutsch, 1949b; Haines and McKeachie, 1967; Julian and Perry, 1967; Wheeler, 1972). In these studies, however, the course examination was given *after* the termination of the cooperative relationship, and the goal structure of the examination was interpersonal competition where students worked alone, did not communicate, and were graded on a curve. Performance in such a competitive situation does not measure achievement under the prior cooperative conditions and is biased in favor of the subjects in the competitive condition. The motivation of students to do well on final examinations, furthermore, would operate to minimize the effects of how discussion groups were structured prior to the examination.

In comparing achievement in cooperative and individualistic situations, the most relevant literature has contrasted individual problem solving with group problem solving. Watson and Johnson (1972) review the results of most studies in this area and conclude that the group problem solving is superior to even the individual work of the most expert persons and is considerably superior to the individual efforts of any randomly selected subject. This body of research clearly indicates that on problem-solving tasks a cooperative goal structure will result in higher achievement than will the use of an individualistic goal structure. A series of studies has demonstrated that children from various socio-economic classes, between the ages of 3 to 11, in classrooms ranging in size from 4 to 17 members, achieve more in such areas as mathematics, vocational development, and reading when they are working under a cooperative goal structure compared to an individualistic one (Mintz, 1951; Hamblin et al., 1971; Hamblin, Hathaway, and Wodarski, 1971; Wodarski, Hamblin, Buckholdt, and Ferritor, 1971, 1973; Buckholdt, Ferritor, and Tucker, 1974). Wodarski and his associates (1973), for example, conducted a study in which they compared student achievement on a series of math problems within cooperative, individualistic, and mixed (partly cooperative and partly individualistic) goal structures. The results clearly demonstrate that student achievement was highest in the cooperative goal structure, next highest in the mixed, and lowest in the individualistic. Both the least and the most mathematically gifted students performed higher in the cooperative conditions than they did in the individualistic conditions.

There is, then, considerable evidence that the most desirable goal structure for promoting achievement in problem-solving (as well as information-recall) tasks is a cooperative one. When working on problem-solving tasks within a cooperative goal structure, students are also learning how to problem solve, how to cooperate, and how to join with other individuals to solve a common problem or to accomplish a common task. Coleman (1972) emphasizes the importance of such learning by stating that the primary intent of schools should be to turn out responsible, productive persons who can participate effectively in cooperative situations. He states that working with others under the discipline imposed by a common task and purpose is incompatible with the individualistic goal of learning around which current schools are organized and that cooperative involvement with others is necessary to provide both a direction to life and the motivation to learn how to implement it.

The use of cooperative goal structures will promote the cognitive beliefs that the subject matter area is important, that the student can affect his achievement in the class, and that the material is not too difficult to master (DeVries, Edwards, and Wells, 1974a). The creativeness of problem solving depends upon the presence of controversy and divergent thinking within a group (D. W. Johnson and F. P. Johnson, 1975); there is evidence that the use of cooperation (compared with competition) promotes divergent thinking within a class (Edwards and DeVries, 1974). Students in a cooperative situation (compared with a competitive one) attach greater importance to academic achievement and believe that their peers have a positive interest in their success in learning (Hulten, 1974).

One of the most important variables in the cognitive domain is the cognitive development of students. The type of cognitive ability focused upon in the research is the ability to take the perspective of other individuals—which is the opposite of an egocentric view of the world. The assumption that there is a basic relationship between cooperation and social perspective taking underlies a great deal of social psychological theorizing. *Social perspective taking* (or role taking) is the ability to understand how a situation appears to another person and how that person is reacting cognitively and emotionally to the situation; it is the ability to put oneself in the place of others and understand their perspective on the situation. *Egocentrism* is defined as the inability to take another person's perspective. Cooperation theorists have posited that being able to take the perspective of other individuals is a basic requirement for cooperative interaction (Asch, 1952; Deutsch, 1949a, 1962; Heider, 1958; Mead, 1934; Nelson and Kagan, 1972; D. W. Johnson, 1974a, 1974c), and theorists in social and cognitive development posit the same relationship (Piaget, 1948; Flavell, 1968; Kohlberg, 1969). The link between cooperation and social perspective taking is important as there is a general positive relationship between social perspective taking and (1) social adjustment (Bell and Hall, 1954; Dymond, 1950; Dymond, Hughes, and Raabe, 1952; Rose, Frankel, and Kerr, 1956; Rotherberg, 1970), (2) the development of the ability to communicate effectively (Flavell, 1968; Krauss and Glucksberg, 1969), (3) autonomous moral judgment (Piaget, 1948; Kohlberg, 1969), (4) personal identity and self-awareness (Mead, 1934; Kinch, 1963), (5) reflective thought to make sense out of one's experiences (Mead, 1934), (6) ability to predict the effects of one's behavior (D. W. Johnson, 1974a), (7) open-mindedness and acceptance of differences (D. W. Johnson and F. P. Johnson, 1975), and (9) empathy (D. W. Johnson, 1971, 1974a). Thus if cooperation is demonstrated to increase a person's social perspective-taking abilities it would be directly linked to the variables listed above. D. W. Johnson (1974a), noting that there was no direct data to validate the proposition that cooperation and social perspective taking are related, conducted a study in which fourth grade students were divided on their disposition to behave in a cooperative or a competitive manner and were examined on ability to take the physical and emotional perspective of other individuals. He found no relationship between ability to take the physical perspective of other individuals and the disposition to cooperate or compete, but a strong relationship was found to exist between disposition to cooperate and ability to take the emotional perspective of other individuals. When compared to fourth graders who were disposed to compete, individuals disposed to cooperate were better able to identify how others are feeling and to explain why they were feeling that way. A subsequent study with fifth graders in a different school system and from a different socio-economic class replicated these findings (D. W. Johnson, 1974c). These results imply that the development of affective perspective-taking abilities may be dependent upon the repeated experiencing of cooperative interaction with other persons. Previous studies by D. W. Johnson (1971) indicate that cooperativeness may be increased when individuals are trained to take the affective and cognitive perspective of others. Thus the use of cooperative goal structures within learning situations may be crucial for cognitive development of students and the reduction of egocentrism necessary for such abilities as social adjustment, communication, autonomous moral judgment based upon mutual reciprocity and justice, reflective thought, empathy, and the productive utilization of differences among persons.

AFFECTIVE OUTCOMES

There have been a number of variables within the affective domain which have been found to be related to the use of cooperative, competitive, and individualistic goal structures. The affective domain includes the feelings, attitudes, and values promoted by instructional activities (D. W. Johnson, 1973a, 1974b). Many of the affective outcome variables are also variables affecting the ways in which students interact and behavior in learning situations. They were mentioned in the section on process variables.

Several studies have shown that students' attitudes toward the instructional activities, tasks, and subject areas will be more positive under cooperative than under competitive goal structures (Deutsch, 1949b; Hammond and Goldman, 1961; Raven and Eachus, 1963; Dunn and Goldman, 1966; Crombag, 1966; Haines and McKeachie, 1967; Edwards and DeVries, 1972, 1974; Wheeler, 1972; Wheeler and Ryan, 1973; R. T. Johnson, 1974; DeVries, Edwards, and Wells, 1974a; Bryant, Crockenberg, and Wilce, 1974; DeVries and Mescon, 1974; Blanchard, Weigel, and Cook, 1974). One study found less satisfaction in a cooperative situation (Shaw, 1958). Another exception to the findings is a study that found that winners had more positive attitudes toward the instructional situation than did losers (Bryant, Crockenberg, and Wilce, 1974). Wheeler (1972) found more positive attitudes toward the teacher when students were structured cooperatively. Attitudes toward other students are much more positive in cooperative than in competitive goal structures; this research was discussed at length in the section on process variables. Finally, *teachers* prefer and have more positive attitudes toward cooperatively structured classrooms after they have experienced them (Weigel, Wiser, and Cook, 1974).

One of the most important social problems facing our country is the prejudice toward groups and individuals who are in some way different from the middle-class white majority. Ethnic groups, the lower and working classes, physically and mentally handicapped individuals, and even the aged are discriminated against because of their "difference." In cooperative, competitive, an individualistic goal structures there is a marked difference in attitudes generated toward heterogeneity in skills, background, characteristics, beliefs, values, culture, and information among the individuals involved. In a cooperative structure, such differences are positively valued as greater resources to help the group accomplish a variety of goals. The studies on goal facilitation demonstrate that a person will value characteristics in others that will facilitate the accomplishment of their mutual goals (D. W. Johnson and S. Johnson, 1972; S. Johnson and D. W. Johnson, 1972). When differences are perceived as being facilitative of goal accomplishment, they will be respected and valued. In a competitive structure, such differences are often perceived as threats (when they provide others with some possible advantage in "winning") or as something to ridicule (when they increase the chances of the others to "lose"). Dunn and Goldman (1966) found that individuals in a cooperative relationship were more accepting of each other than were individuals in a competitive relationship. Deutsch (1949b) found more diversity in amount of contributions per member in cooperative groups. Thus the use of a cooperative instructional structure will implicitly teach the values of respecting and valuing differences among individuals.

The use of cooperative interracial groups has frequently been suggested as a way to create greater interracial cooperation and acceptance (Allport, 1954; Gottlieb, 1965; Thelen, 1970; Watson and Johnson, 1972). Yet studies of temporary ad hoc groups that meet for a couple of hours, find no increases in interracial communication among members of cooperative as compared to competitive groups (Katz, Goldston, and Benjamin, 1958; Katz and Benjamin, 1960; Cohen, 1969). When groups have members from different racial or ethnic groups, it is important that the goal be clearly cooperative, the members be of equal status, the interracial cooperation be rewarded and supported by the teacher, and the groups meet long enough for the members to have a prolonged experience in working with one another. Under these conditions there are a number of studies that demonstrate that interracial contact will produce positive attitude change (Katz, 1955; Singer, 1967; Cook, 1969, 1971; Harding, et al., 1969; Witte, 1972; DeVries and Edwards, 1972; Cohen, 1973; Weigel, Wiser, and Cook, 1974; Blanchard, Weigel, and Cook, 1974). Harding and his associates (1969), in reviewing the research on interethnic prejudice, cite well over two dozen studies conducted in educational, residential, and occupational settings that support the proposition that cooperative, equal status contact that is supported by authority figures will produce positive attitude changes toward minority ethnic group members. Witte (1972), using groups that met for a college semester, found that membership in a group with a cooperative goal structure created more interracial peer tutoring, more racial acceptance, and less racial isolation. DeVries and Edwards (1972) found that the use of cooperative groups in a math class resulted in more cross-race choices on both friendship and mutual helping, compared to math classes structured competitively. Weigel, Wiser, and Cook (1974) found that the use of cooperatively structured groups in English classes (compared to competitively structured classes) resulted in dramatically lower cross-race conflicts, dramatically higher cross-race helping and tutoring, and greater cross-race friendships and attraction. The promotion of positive interracial attitudes and behaviors is especially marked when the cooperative groups experience success (as opposed to failure) and when a black teammate is not markedly incompetent (Ashmore, 1970; Blanchard, Adelman, and Cook, 1974; Blanchard, Weigel, and Cook, 1974). These studies support the notion that the use of a cooperative goal structure will result in the acceptance and appreciation of differences among students.

It follows from the definitions of cooperation and competition that there will be differences in the amount of failure experienced by students in the two different goal structures. Since every group member contributes in some way to accomplishing the goal, all individuals in a cooperative structure potentially will have a success experience. But, since there can be only one "winner" in a competitive goal structure, the vast majority of students will experience failure. This is an important difference in outcomes. Although there is no experimental research on the effects of prolonged failure experience, it seems reasonable to assume that a person's self-attitudes and feelings of competence will be affected. In the traditional competitive classroom, the purpose of classroom evaluation is to rank students from the "best" to the "worst." In most classrooms, fairly stable patterns of achievement exist so that the majority of students always "lose" and a few students always "win." Thus, a student may spend twelve years in public schools being confronted daily with the fact that he is a "loser." If the student desires to "win," the daily frustration of failing may be a concomitant of schooling. A sense of helplessness, worthlessness, and incompetence may result from such a situation.

Hurlock (1927) found in an experiment with children that members of a group that was defeated on the first of four days of competition never overcame their initial failure and attained inferior scores for the entire duration of the experiment, even though the groups had been matched on the basis of ability. Tseng (1969) found that as rewards increase in value, so do the tension and frustration of failure; children who failed in competitive situations performed poorly in subsequent competitions. Crockenberg, Bryant, and Wilce (1974) found that while winners in a competitive learning situation were almost unanimously fully satisfied with their experiences, nonwinners perceived their learning experience as boring, unfair, and not fun, and perceived themselves negatively; male nonwinners perceived the learning situation as unpleasant. Overall their findings showed much stronger reactions by males than by females. Atkinson (1965) predicted from his theory of achievement motivation that the student who chronically experiences failure would become primarily oriented toward avoiding failure (thus becoming nonachievement oriented). The tendency to avoid failure inhibits the student from attempting a task on which he is to be evaluated, especially when the probability of success is intermediate. Students, however, are forced into achievement-oriented situations. The student who is dominated by a tendency to avoid failure is likely to choose tasks with a very high or a very low chance of success. Doing so minimizes his anxiety about failure, for if the chance of success is very high he is almost sure not to fail, and when the chance for success is very low no one can blame him for failure. Failure reduces the attraction felt towards one's classmates (Ashmore, 1970; Blanchard, Adelman, and Cook, 1974).

A large number of educators, psychologists, and popular writers have challenged the notion that it must be an inevitable part of American education that a large proportion of students experience failure (Holt, 1964; Kagan, 1965; Nesbit, 1967; Jackson, 1968; Glasser, 1969; Kohl, 1969; Postman and Weingartner, 1969, D. W. Johnson, 1970; Rathbone, 1970; Rogers, 1970; Wilhels, 1970; Illich, 1971; Silberman, 1971; Walberg and Thomas, 1971; D. W. Johnson and R. T. Johnson, 1974). Walberg and Thomas (1971) state that competition does not contribute effectively to learning. Holt (1969) states that for the student the most interesting thing in the classroom is the other students, but in a competitive goal structure the student must ignore them, act as if these other students, all about him, only a few feet away, are really not there. He cannot interact with them, talk with, smile at them, often he cannot even look at them. In many schools he cannot talk to other students in the halls between classes; in many schools he cannot talk to other students during lunch. Holt states that this is splendid training for a world in which, when you are not studying the other person to figure out how to do him in, you pay no attention to him.

One probable and undesirable affective outcome of a pervasive competitive situation is that individuals will try to obstruct each other's goal accomplishment, and they will dislike behaviors that facilitate another person's goal accomplishment. They will have hostile and angry feelings toward individuals who "win," thus relegating them to failure, or will become angry at the teacher, at the school, or at themselves (which will be expressed in such ways as depression, self-punishment, withdrawal, or self-destructiveness). Kagan (1965) notes that individuals who are vulnerable to guilt over hostile thoughts and feelings toward others may become anxious when placed in a competitive structure and have inhibitions about their competitiveness, thereby reducing their chances for success. Furthermore, students who are sensitive to their peers' rejection may fear the consequences of winning and thus not achieve up to their potential.

Even when a student is one of the few individuals who experience success most of the time, an emphasis upon competition can have long-term destructive consequences. If a student is continually reinforced and given attention and approval for "winning," he may believe that a person is valued only for his "wins" and not for what he is as a person. The result of this belief is a need to continually prove his value through achievement. There is a basic rejection of the student as a person in such a process.

One of the most interesting discussions of the destructiveness of competition was written by Bertrand Russell (1930). He notes that the "rat race" in American life does not have its origin in people's fears that they will fail to get their breakfast the next morning but rather in their fears that they will fail to outshine their neighbors. The lives of many individuals seem to have the psychology of the 100-yard dash, and they remain too anxious and concentrated upon "winning" to be happy. All the quieter pleasures become abandoned. Russell sees such an emphasis upon competition as a general decay of civilized standards. He believes that the competitive philosophy of life, which views life as a contest in which respect is to be accorded to the victor, breeds a dinosaur cycle, where intelligence is ignored for strength and finally where the powerful (but stupid) kill each other off, leaving the world for the intelligent bystanders. Being sterile because of high anxiety over success is an example of such selective evolution.

For the teacher who is truly interested in intellectual functioning, one of the saddest probable consequences of the continual use of competitive goal structures is that the intrinsic motivation for learning and thinking will become subverted. A highly competitive person does not learn for intrinsic reasons; learning is a means to an end, the end being "winning." Intellectual pursuit for itself becomes unheard of; knowledge that does not help one "win" becomes a waste of time. Thus Leonard (1968) states that when learning becomes truly rewarding for its own sake, competition will be seen to be irrelevant to the learning process and damaging to the development of free-ranging, lifelong learners. Neill (1960) states that to get the better of another person is "a damnable objective"; he believes that when the child's natural interest in things is considered, one begins to realize the destructiveness of competition for rewards or for the avoidance of punishments. For Neill, true interest is the life force of the whole personality, and such interest is completely spontaneous and cannot be compelled through competitive goal structures.

APPENDIX B
diagnostic and
instructional exercises

In order to facilitate the development of cooperative, competitive, and individualistic skills and in order to diagnose present dispositions of students, you may give your students specific tasks for instructional and diagnostic purposes. In this appendix we shall review two tasks that have been used in research studies on cooperation and competition to diagnose the predisposition of persons to corporate or compete. For a detailed discussion of exercises for teaching cooperative skills and attitudes, see D. W. Johnson (1972) and D. W. Johnson and F. P. Johnson (1975).

MARBLE-PULL EXERCISE

Madsen (1971) developed the Marble-Pull Task to assess predisposition in young children toward cooperation or competition. In this task, two children face each other across a table. Each holds a string attached to a wooden marble holder that will move in either direction on a wooden board, depending on which string is pulled. The object of the game is to slide the wooden holder so that the marble will drop into a hole at either end of the board. In order to get the marble into a hole one child has to relax his string while the other child pulls. If both children pull at the same time, the marble holder separates and neither child can then pull the marble to a hole. A picture of this situation appears below.

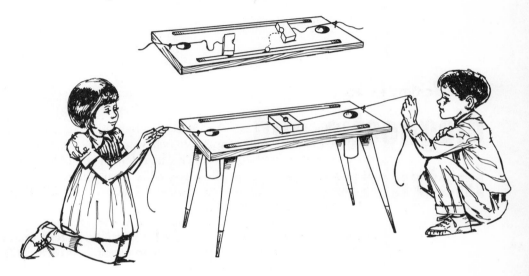

marble-pull apparatus

Tell the students that they will win two points for each marble they get in their respective holes. The points will be exchanged for prizes after the game is finished. The procedure for getting a marble into one's hole should be described and what happens when both students pull on their strings at the same time should be demonstrated. When both students understand what happens when both pull on their strings and when only one pulls on his or her string, the game begins. Tell the students that they can talk to each other as they play the game. Give the students ten tries at the game, recording the outcome on a sheet of paper. Then inform each student of how many points he or she has earned and give them a prize.

In this game a competitive person will never let his opponent win. A cooperative person will relax his string so that the other player can pull the marble to the other player's hole. The cooperative solution to the game is to have students alternate so that each receives ten points, that is, each pulls the marble into his hole five times. The cooperativeness of the student is indicated by the number of times he lets the other player get the marble.

For older students, the Prisoner's Dilemma Game given in Johnson (1972) can be used; the number of cooperative or competitive choices can be used to measure the person's predisposition to cooperate or compete.

Marble-Pull Task

	Own	Other	Neither
Marble in hole	_____	_____	_____

CHOICE CARDS EXERCISE

The Choice Cards Task was developed by Kagan and Madsen (1972) to study cooperative and competitive behavior among elementary school children. It may be used, however, with high school students. The choice cards to be used are illustrated in Figure B-2. Two different sets of the cards should be used, one with the cooperative alternative on the left and one with the cooperative alternative on the right.

The procedure for using the cards is as follows. First, place two students at a table facing each other. Instruct them that they will play a game in which each is required to choose one side of each card; they then receive the number of checkers nearest them on the chosen side of the card. In Card 1, for example, if the chooser indicated the right side of the card he would receive two checkers and the other player would receive one. The checkers may be traded in on prizes after the game, with the number of checkers determining the quality of the prize. First one player goes through the cards and makes the choices, and then the other player goes through the cards and makes the choices. Flip a coin to see which student goes first. Then shuffle the cards. Take the top card and place it in front of the chooser, placing black checkers on the spots nearest the student and red checkers on the spots farthest away from the chooser. Tell the chooser to select either the right or left side of the card, take his checkers from the card, and then place the other player's checkers in front of the other player. Record which side of the card the student chose (cooperative or competitive). Repeat this procedure for each card. Then reshuffle the cards and repeat the procedure with the *same* student. Finally, repeat the entire procedure twice with the other student.

From this game a score of cooperativeness or competitiveness can be obtained by simply noting the frequency of each type of choice. Students may then be ranked on the basis of most cooperative to most competitive.

	Left*	Right
1		
2		
3		
4		

	Left	Right*
1a		
2a		
3a		
4a		

The left choice is cooperative in the pictures of the cards below; when the reverse set of cards is made, the right choice will be cooperative.

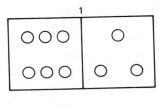

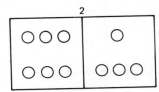

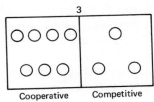
Cooperative   Competitive

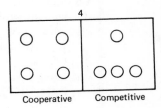
Cooperative   Competitive

bibliography

ALLPORT, G. 1954. *The nature of prejudice.* Cambridge, Mass.: Addison-Wesley Publishing Co.

ALMACK, J. C. 1930. Mental efficiency of consulting pairs. *Educational Research Bulletin* 9:2–3.

ANDERSON, H. H. 1939. Domination and integration in the social behavior of kindergarten children in an experimental play situation. *Genetic Psychology Monographs* 2:357–85.

ASCH, S. E. 1952. *Social Psychology.* Englewood Cliffs, N. J.: Prentice-Hall.

ASHMORE, R. D. 1970. Solving the problems of prejudice. In B. E. Collins, ed., *Social Psychology.* Reading, Mass.: Addison-Wesley Publishing Co.

ATKINSON, J. W. 1965. The mainsprings of achievement-oriented activity. In J. D. Krumholtz, ed., *Learning and the Educational Process,* pp. 25–66. Chicago: Rand McNally & Co.

ATKINSON, J. W., and J. O. RAYNOR. 1974. Motivation and achievement. Washington, D.C.: Winston & Sons.

BAKER, E. H. 1968. A pre-civil war simulation for teaching American history. In S. S. Boocock and E. O. Schild, eds., *Simulation Games in Learning.* Beverly Hills, Calif.: Sage.

BANDURA, A., D. ROSS, and S. A. ROSS. 1963. Imitation of film-mediated aggressive models. *Journal of Abnormal and Social Psychology* 66:3–11.

BELL, G. B., and H. E. HALL. 1954. The relationship between leadership and empathy. *Journal of Abnormal and Social Psychology* 49:156–57.

BERKOWITZ, L., and L. R. DANIELS. 1963. Responsibility and dependency. *Journal of Abnormal and Social Psychology* 66:429–36.

BLAKE, R. R., and J. S. MOUTON. 1961. Comprehension of own and out-group positions under intergroup competition. *Journal of Conflict Resolution* 5:304–10.

————. 1962. The intergroup dynamics of win-lose conflict and problem-solving collaboration in union-management relations. In M. Sherif, ed., *Intergroup Relations and Leadership,* pp. 94–140. New York: John Wiley.

BLANCHARD, F. A., L. ADELMAN, and S. W. COOK. 1974. The effect of group success and failure upon interpersonal attraction in cooperating interracial groups. *Journal of Personality and Social Psychology.* In press.

BLANCHARD, F. A., R. H. WEIGEL, and S. W. COOK. 1974. The effect of relative competence of group members upon interpersonal attraction in cooperating interracial groups. Mimeographed report, University of Colorado, submitted for publication.

BLAU, P. M. 1954. Cooperation and competition in a bureaucracy. *American Journal of Sociology* 59:530–35.

BONOMA, T. V., J. T. TEDESCHI, and B. HELM. 1974. Some effects of target cooperation and reciprocated promises on conflict resolution. *Sociometry* 37:251–61.

BRODEN, M., R. V. HALL, and B. MITTS. 1971. The effect of self-recording on the classroom behavior of two eighth grade students. *Journal of Applied Behavior Analysis* 4:191–200.

BRUNER, J. S. 1966. *Toward a Theory of Instruction*. Cambridge: Harvard University Press.

BRYANT, B. K., and S. B. CROCKENBERG. 1974. Cooperative and competitive environments. *Catalog of Selected Documents in Psychology*, 4:53.

BRYANT, B. K., S. B. CROCKENBERG, and L. S. WILCE. 1974. The educational context for the study of cooperation and helpful concern for others. Paper presented at the convention of the AERA, Chicago, April.

BUCKHOLDT, D. R., D. E. FERRITOR, and S. TUCKER. 1974. Effects of training in tutoring and shared group consequences on reading performance and tutoring behaviors. Paper presented at the AERA, Chicago, April.

BURNSTEIN, E., and P. WORCHEL. 1962. Arbitrariness of frustration and its consequences for aggression in a social situation. *Journal of Personality* 30:528–40.

CHAPMAN, J. R., and R. B. FEDER. 1917. The effect of external incentives on improvement. *Journal of Educational Psychology* 8:469–74.

CLAYTON, D. 1964. Competition motivates typewriting students. *The Balance Sheet* (December).

CLIFFORD, M. M. 1971. Motivational effects of competition and goal-setting in reward and nonreward conditions. *Journal of Experimental Education* 39:

COHEN, E. G. 1969. Interracial interaction disability. Unpublished manuscript, Stanford University.

———. 1973. Modifying the effects of social structure. *American Behavioral Scientist* 16:861–79.

COLEMAN, J. S. 1959. Academic achievement and the structure of competition. *Harvard Educational Review* 29:339–51.

———. 1972. The children have outgrown the schools. *Psychology Today* 5 (February):72–75.

COOK, S. W. 1969. Motives in a conceptual analysis of attitude-related behavior. In W. J. Arnold and D. Levine eds., *Nebraska Symposium on Motivation*. Lincoln, Nebraska: University of Nebraska Press, 179–231.

———. 1971. The effect of unintended contact upon racial interaction and attitude change. Final report, U. S. Office of Education, Project #5–1320.

CROCKENBERG, S., and B. BRYANT. 1973. Helping and sharing behavior in cooperative and competitive classrooms. Paper presented at the meetings of the Society on Research in Child Development, Philadelphia, March.

———, and L. S. WILCE. 1974. The effects of cooperatively and competitively structured learning environments on intrapersonal behavior. Paper presented at the annual meeting of the APA, New Orleans, September.

CROMBAG, H. F. 1966. Cooperation and competition in means-interdependent triads. *Journal of Personality and Social Psychology* 4:692–95.

DECI, E. L. 1971. Effects of externally mediated rewards on intrinsic motivation. *Journal of Personality and Social Psychology* 18:105–15.

DEUTSCH, M. 1949a. A theory of cooperation and competition. *Human Relations* 2:129–52.

———. 1949b. An experimental study of the effects of cooperation and competition upon group process. *Human Relations* 2:199–232.

———. 1958. Trust and suspicion. *Journal of Conflict Resolution* 2:265–79.

———. 1960. The effect of motivational orientation upon trust and suspicion. *Human Relations* 13:123–39.

———. 1962. Cooperation and trust: some theoretical notes. In M. R. Jones, ed., *Nebraska Symposium on Motivation*, pp. 275–320. Lincoln, Neb.: University of Nebraska Press.

———., and R. KRAUSS. 1962. Studies of interpersonal bargaining. *Journal of Conflict Resolution* 6:52–76.

DEVRIES, D. L., and K. J. EDWARDS. 1972a. Student teams and instructional games: their effects on cross-race and cross-sex interaction. Center Report #173, Center for Social Organization of Schools, Johns Hopkins University.

———. 1972b. Learning games and student teams: their effects on classroom processes. Center Report #142, Center for Social Organization of Schools, Johns Hopkins University.

———. 1973. Learning games and student teams: their effects on classroom process. *American Educational Research Journal* 10:307–18.

———. 1974. Cooperation in the classroom: towards a theory of alternative reward-task classroom structures. Paper presented at the annual meeting of the American Educational Research Association, Chicago, April.

———, and E. H. WELLS. 1974a. Teams-games-tournament in the social studies classroom: effects on academic achievement, student attitudes, cognitive beliefs, and classroom climate. Report # 173, Center for Social Organization of Schools, Johns Hopkins University.

———. 1974b. Team competition effects on classroom group process. Report #174, Center for Social Organization of Schools, Johns Hopkins University.

———, and G. M. FENNESSEY. 1973. Using teams-games-tournament (TGT) in the classroom. Center for Social Organization of Schools, Johns Hopkins University.

DEVRIES, D., and I. MESCON. 1974. Using TGT at the Moses DeWitt elementary school: a preliminary report. Mimeographed report, Center for Social Organization of Schools, Johns Hopkins University.

DEVRIES, D. L., D. MUSE, and E. H. WELLS. 1971. The effects on students of working in cooperative groups: an exploratory study. Center Report #120, Center for Social Organization of Schools, Johns Hopkins University.

DREEBEN, R. 1968. *On What is Learned in School*. Reading, Mass.: Addison-Wesley.

DUNN, R. E., and M. GOLDMAN. 1966. Competition and noncompetition in relationship to satisfaction and feelings toward own group and nongroup members. *Journal of Social Psychology* 68:299–311.

DYMOND, R. Personality and empathy. 1950. *Journal of Consulting Psychology* 14:343–50.

————, A. HUGHES, and V. RABBE. 1952. Measurable changes in empathy with age. *Journal of Consulting Psychology* 16:202–6.

EDWARDS, K. J., and D. L. DEVRIES. 1972. Learning games and student teams: their effects on student attitudes and achievement. Center Report #147, Center for Social Organization of Schools, Johns Hopkins University.

————, 1974. The effects of teams-games-tournament and two instructional variations on classroom process, student attitudes, and student achievement. Report #172, Center for Social Organization of Schools, Johns Hopkins University.

————, and John P. Snyder. 1972. Games and teams. *Simulation And Games* 3:247–69.

FARB, P. 1963. *Ecology.* New York: Time, Inc.

FAY, A. S. 1970. The effects of cooperation and competition on learning and recall. Unpublished master's thesis, George Peabody College.

FESTINGER, L. 1950. Informal social communication. *Psychological Review* 57:271–82.

————. 1954. A theory of social comparison processes. *Human Relations* 7:117–40.

FIEDLER, F. E. 1967. Effect of intergroup competition on group member adjustment. *Personnel Psychology* 20:30–44.

FLAVELL, J. H. 1968. *The Development of Role-Taking and Communication Skills in Children.* New York: John Wiley & Sons.

FRENCH, J. R. P., JR. 1951. Group productivity. In H. Guetzkow, ed., *Groups, Leadership and Men,* pp. 44–55. Pittsburgh: Carnegie Press.

GLASSER, W. 1969. *Schools Without Failure.* New York: Harper & Row.

GORANSON, R. E., and L. BERKOWITZ. 1966. Reciprocity and responsibility reactions to prior help. *Journal of Personality and Social Psychology* 3:227–32.

GOTTHEIL, E. 1955. Changes in social perceptions contingent upon competing or cooperating. *Sociometry* 18:132–37.

GOTTLIEB, D. 1965. School integration and absorption of newcomers. *Integrated Education* 3.

GREENBERG, P. J. 1932. Competition in children: an experimental study. *American Journal of Psychology* 44:221–48.

GROSSACK, M. 1954. Some effects of cooperating and competition upon small group behavior. *Journal of Abnormal and Social Psychology* 49:341–48.

GURNEE, H. 1968. Learning under competitive and collaborative sets. *Journal of Experimental Social Psychology* 4:26–34.

HAEFNER, D., P. LANGHAM, H. AXELROD, and J. T. LANZETTA. 1954. Some effects of situational threat on group behavior. *Journal of Abnormal and Social Psychology* 49:445–53.

HAINES, D. B., and W. J. MCKEACHIE. 1967. Cooperative versus competitive discussion methods in teaching introductory psychology. *Journal of Educational Psychology* 58:386–90.

HAMBLIN, R. L., D. BUCKHOLDT, D. FERRITOR, M. KOZLOFF, and L. BLACKWELL. 1971. *The Humanization Processes.* New York: Wiley.

HAMBLIN, R. L., C. HATHAWAY, and J. S. WODARSKI. 1971. Group contingencies, peer tutoring, and accelerating academic achievement. In E. Ramp and B. Hopkins, eds., *A New Direction for Education: Behavior Analysis.* Lawrence, Kansas: The University of Kansas, Department of Human Development, 41–53.

HAMMOND, L., and M. GOLDMAN. 1961. Competition and non-competition and its relationship to individual and group productivity. *Sociometry* 24:46–60.

HARDING, J., H. PROSHANSKY, B. KUTNER, and I. CHEIN. 1969. Prejudice and ethnic relations. In G. Lindzey and E. Aronson, eds., *Handbook of Social Psychology*, vol. V. Reading, Mass.: Addison-Wesley.

HARVEY, O. J. 1956. An experimental investigation of negative and positive relations between small groups through judgmental indices. *Sociometry* 19:201–9.

HEIDER, F. 1958. *The Psychology of Interpersonal Relations.* New York: John Wiley & Sons.

HENRY, J. 1963. *Culture Against Man.* New York: Random House.

HOLT, J. 1964. *How Children Fail.* New York: Dell Publishing Co.

———. 1969. *The Underachieving School.* New York: Dell Publishing Co.

HULTEN, B. H. 1974. Games and teams: an effective combination in the classroom. Paper presented at the AERA Convention, Chicago, April.

HUMPHREY, J. H. 1967. The use of the active game learning medium in the reinforcement of reading skills with fourth grade children. *Journal of Special Education* 1:369–73.

HURLOCK, E. B. 1927. Use of group rivalry as an incentive. *Journal of Abnormal and Social Psychology* 22:278–90.

HUSBAND, R. W. 1940. Cooperation versus solitary problem solving. *Journal of Social Psychology* 11:405–9.

ILLICH, I. 1971. *Deschooling Society.* New York: Harrow Books.

JACKSON, P. W. 1968. *Life in Classrooms.* New York: Holt, Rinehart & Winston.

JOHNSON, D. W. 1970. *The Social Psychology of Education.* New York: Holt, Rinehart, & Winston.

———. 1971. Role reversal: a summary and review of the research. *International Journal of Group Tensions* 1:318–34.

———. 1972. *Reaching Out: Interpersonal Effectiveness and Self-Actualization.* Englewood Cliffs, N. J.: Prentice-Hall.

———. 1973a. Student attitudes toward cooperation and competition in a midwestern school district. Unpublished report, University of Minnesota.

———. 1973b. *Contemporary Social Psychology.* Philadelphia: Lippincott.

———. 1973c. The affective side of the schooling experience. *Elementary School Journal* 73:306–13.

———. 1973d. Communication in conflict situations: a critical review of the research. *International Journal of Group Tensions* 3:46–67.

———. 1974a. Cooperativeness and social perspective taking. *Journal of Personality and Social Psychology.* In press.

———. 1974b. Evaluating affective outcomes of schools. In H. J. Walberg, ed., *Evaluating School Performance.* Berkeley: McCutchan Publishing Corp.

————. 1974c. Affective perspective taking and cooperative predisposition. Mimeographed report, University of Minnesota. Submitted for publication.

JOHNSON, D. W. 1974d. A theory of social effectiveness. In M. Wong, ed., *Why Drugs: The Psychology of Drug Abuse.* Minneapolis: University of Minnesota.

————, and F. P. JOHNSON. 1975a. *Joining Together: Group Theory and Group Skills.* Englewood Cliffs, N. J.: Prentice-Hall.

JOHNSON, D. W., and R. T. JOHNSON. 1974a. Instructional structure: cooperative, competitive, or individualistic. *Review of Eductional Research* 44:213–40.

————. 1974b. The goal structure of open schools. *Journal of Research and Development in Education,* in press.

————. 1974c. Effects of cooperative, competitive, and individualized goal structures on learning outcomes. Paper presented at the annual meeting of the American Psychological Association, New Orleans, September.

JOHNSON, D. W., and S. JOHNSON. 1972. The effects of attitude similarity, expectation of goal facilitation, and actual goal facilitation on interpersonal attraction. *Journal of Experimental Social Psychology* 8:197–206.

JOHNSON, D. W., and R. J. LEWICKI. 1969. The initiation of superordinate goals. *Journal of Applied Behavioral Science* 5:9–24.

JOHNSON, D. W., and R. MATROSS. 1975. Attitude change methods of helping people change. In F. H. Kanfer and A. P. Goldstein, eds., *Helping People Change: Methods and Materials.* Elmsford, N. Y.: Pergamon Press.

JOHNSON, R. T. 1972. Cooperation in the elementary science classroom: perception and preferences of sixth grade students. University of Minnesota, Mimeographed report.

————. 1974. Perceptions and preferences toward cooperation and competition in elementary science classes. Mimeographed report, University of Minnesota.

————, D. W. JOHNSON, and B. BRYANT. 1973. Cooperation and competition in the classroom: perceptions and preferences as related to students' feelings of personal control. *Elementary School Journal* 73:306–13.

JOHNSON, S., and D. W. JOHNSON. 1972. The effects of other's actions, attitude similarity, and race on attraction towards others. *Human Relations,* 25:121–30.

JONES, S. C., and V. H. VROOM. 1964. Division of labor and performance under cooperative-competitive conditions. *Journal of Abnormal Social Psychology* 68:313–20.

JULIAN, J. W., D. W. BISHOP, and F. E. FIEDLER. 1966. Quasi-therapeutic effects of intergroup competition. *Journal of Personality and Social Psychology* 3:321–27.

JULIAN, J. W., and F. A. PERRY. 1967. Cooperation contrasted with intra-group and inter-group competition. *Sociometry* 30:79–90.

KAGAN, J. 1965. Personality and the learning process. *Daedalus* (Summer) 553–63.

KAGAN, S., and M. C. MADSEN. 1971. Cooperation and competition of Mexican, Mexican-American, and Anglo-American children of two ages under four instructional sets. *Developmental Psychology* 5:32–39.

————. 1972. Rivalry in Anglo-American and Mexican children of two ages. *Journal of Personality and Social Psychology* 24:214–20.

KATZ, I. 1955. *Conflict and Harmony in an Adolescent Interracial Group.* New York: New York University Press.

————, J. GOLDSTON, and L. BENJAMIN. 1958. Behavior and productivity in biracial work groups. *Human Relations* 11:123–41.

KATZ, I., and L. BENJAMIN. 1960. Effects of white authoritarianism in biracial work groups. *Journal of Abnormal and Social Psychology* 61:448–56.

KELLEY, H. H., and A. J. STAHELSKI. 1970. Social interaction basis of cooperators' and competitors' beliefs about others. *Journal of Personality and Social Psychology* 16:66–91.

KELLEY, H. H., and J. W. THIBAUT. 1969. Group problem solving. In G. Lindzey and E. Aronson, eds., *The Handbook of Social Psychology,* vol. 4, pp. 1–101. Reading, Mass.: Addison-Wesley Publishing Co.

KINCH, J. W. 1963. A formalized theory of the self-concept. *The American Journal of Sociology* 68:481–86.

KOGAN, N., and M. A. WALLACH. 1967. Risk taking as a function of the situation, the person, and the group. In G. Mandler, P. Mussen, N. Kogan, and M. A. Wallach, *New Directions in Psychology,* vol. 3, pp. 224–66. New York: Holt, Rinehart & Winston.

KOHL, H. R. 1969. *The Open Classroom.* New York: Vintage Books.

KOHLBERG, L. 1969. Stage and sequence: the cognitive-developmental approach to socialization. In D. A. Goslin, ed., *Handbook of Socialization Theory and Research,* pp. 347–480. Chicago: Rand McNally & Co.

KOZOL, J. 1972. The open schoolroom: new words for old deceptions. *Ramparts* 11 (July):38–41.

KRAUSS, R. M. 1966. Structural and attitudinal factors in interpersonal bargaining. *Journal of Experimental Social Psychology* 2:42–55.

————, and M. DEUTSCH. 1966. Communication in interpersonal bargaining. *Journal of Personality and Social Psychology* 4:572–77.

KRAUSS, R. M., and S. GLUCKSBERG. 1969. The development of communication competence as a function of age. *Child Development* 40:255–66.

KRUGMAN, S. F. 1944. Cooperation versus individual efficiency in problem solving. *Journal of Educational Psychology* 35:91–100.

LAUGHLIN, P. R., and R. P. MCGLYNN. 1967. Cooperative versus competitive concept attainment as a function of sex and stimulus display. *Journal of Social Psychology* 7:498–501.

LEONARD, G. B. 1968. *Education and Ecstasy.* New York: Dell Publishing Co.

LEWIN, K. 1935. *A Dynamic Theory of Personality.* New York: McGraw-Hill.

MADSEN, M. C. 1967. Cooperative and competitive motivation of children in three Mexican subcultures. *Psychological Reports* 20:1307–20.

————. 1971. Developmental and cross-cultural differences in cooperative and competitive behavior of young children. *Journal of Cross-Cultural Psychology* 2:365–71.

————, and C. CONNOR. 1973. Cooperative and competitive behavior of retarded and nonretarded children at two ages. *Child Development* 44:175–78.

MADSEN, M. C., and A. SHAPIRA. 1970. Cooperative and competitive behavior of urban Afro-American, Anglo-American, Mexican-American, and Mexican village children. *Developmental Psychology* 3:16–20.

MALLER, J. B. 1929. *Cooperation and Competition.* New York: Teachers College Press.

MASTERS, J. 1972. Effects of social comparison upon the imitation of neutral and altruistic behaviors by young children. *Child Development,* 1972, 43:131–42.

MCCLINTOCK, C. G., and S. P. MCNEEL. 1967. Prior dyadic experience and monetary reward as determinants of cooperative and competitive game behavior. *Journal of Personality and Social Psychology* 5:282–94.

MEAD, G. H. 1934. *Mind, Self, and Society.* Chicago: University of Chicago Press, 1934.

MILLER, A. G., and R. THOMAS. 1972. Cooperation and competition among Blackfoot Indian and urban Canadian children. *Child Development* 43:1104–10.

MILLER, L. K., and R. L. HAMBLIN. 1963. Interdependence, differential rewarding, and productivity. *American Sociological Review* 28:768–78.

MINTZ, A. 1951. Nonadaptive group behavior. *Journal of Abnormal and Social Psychology* 46:150–59.

MISES, LUDWIG VON. 1949. *Human Action: A Treatise on Economics.* New Haven: Yale University Press.

MONTAGU, A. 1965. *The Human Revolution.* New York: World Publishing Company.

———, 1966. *On Being Human.* New York: Hawthorn Books.

MYERS, A. E. 1962a. Team competition, success, and adjustment of group members. *Journal of Abnormal and Social Psychology* 65:325–32.

———. 1962b. Competitive team golf with schizophrenics. Technical Report No. 14. University of Illinois, Group Effectiveness Research Laboratory.

NAUGHT, G. M., and S. F. NEWMAN. 1966. The effect of anxiety on motor steadiness in competitive and non-competitive conditions. *Psychonomic Science* 6:519–20.

NEILL, A. S. 1960. *Summerhill.* New York: Hart Publishing Co.

NELSON, L. L. 1970. The development of cooperation and competition in children from ages five to ten years old: effects of sex, situational determinants, and prior experiences. Doctoral dissertation, University Microfilms, Ann Arbor, Michigan, #71-669.

———, and S. KAGAN. 1972. Competition: the star-spangled scramble. *Psychology Today* 6 (September): 53.

NESBITT, M. 1967. A *Public School for Tomorrow.* New York: A Delta Book.

O'CONNELL, E. J. 1965. Effect of cooperative and competitive set on the learning of imitation. *Journal of Experimental Social Psychology* 1:172–83.

OGILVIE, B. C., and T. A. TUTKO. 1971. Sport: if you want to build character, try something else. *Psychology Today* 5 (October):60–63.

OKUN, M. A., and I. J. DIVESTA. 1974. Cooperation and competition in co-acting groups. *Journal of Personality and Social Psychology.* In press.

OSGOOD, C. E., G. J. SUCI, and P. H. TANNENBAUM. 1957. *The Measurement of Meaning.* Urbana: University of Illinois Press.

PATERSON, T. T. 1955. *Morale in War and Work.* London: Max Parrish.

PETTIGREW, T. F. 1967. Social evaluation theory: convergences and applications. In D. Levine, ed., *Nebraska Symposium on Motivation,* pp. 241–326. Lincoln: University of Nebraska Press.

PHILLIPS, B. N. 1954. An experimental study of the effects of cooperation and competition, intelligence, and cohesiveness on the task efficiency and process behavior of small groups. Unpublished doctoral dissertation, Indiana University.

PHILLIPS, B. W., and L. A. D'AMICO. 1956. Effects of cooperation and competition on the cohesiveness of small face-to-face groups. *Journal of Educational Psychology* 47:65–70.

PIAGET, J. 1948. *The Moral Judgment of the Child.* Glencoe, Ill.: Free Press.

POSTMAN, N., and C. WEINGARTNER. 1969. *Teaching as a Subversive Activity.* New York: Delacorte Press.

RATHBONE, C. H. 1970. Open education and the teacher. Unpublished doctoral dissertation, Harvard University.

RAVEN, B. H., and H. T. EACHUS. 1963. Cooperation and competition in means-interdependent triads. *Journal of Abnormal Social Psychology* 67:307–16.

ROGERS, V. R. 1970. *Teaching in the British Primary Schools.* London: MacMillan and Co.

ROSE, G., N. FRANKEL, and W. KERR. 1956. Empathic and sociometric status among teenagers. *Journal of Genetic Psychology* 89:277–78.

ROTHENBERG, B. B. 1970. Children's social sensitivity and the relationship to interpersonal competence, intrapersonal comfort, and intellectual level. *Developmental Psychology* 2:335–50.

RUSSELL, B. 1930. *The Conquest of Happiness.* New York: Horace Liveright. Reprint. New York: Bantam Books, 1958.

RYAN, F. L., and R. WHEELER. 1973. Relative effects of two environments on the way a simulation game is played by elementary school students. Paper presented at the AERA meeting, New Orleans, February 26.

SCOTT, W. E., and D. J. CHERRINGTON. 1974. The effects of competitive, cooperative, and individualistic reinforcement contingencies. *Journal of Personality and Social Psychology.* In press.

SECORD, P. F., and C. W. BACKMAN. 1964. Interpersonal congruency, perceived similarity and friendship. *Sociometry* 27:115:27.

SHAPIRA, A., and M. C. MADSEN. 1969. Cooperative and competitive behavior of kibbutz and urban children in Israel. *Child Development* 40:609–17.

SHAW, M. E. 1958. Some motivational factors in cooperation and competition. *Journal of Personality* 26:155–69.

SHERIF, M. 1966. *In Common Predicament.* Boston: Houghton Mifflin Co.

———, and C. SHERIF. 1953. *Group in Harmony and Tension.* New York: Harper.

SHERIF, M., O. J. HARVEY, D. J. WHITE, W. R. HOOD, and C. W. SHERIF. 1961. *Intergroup Conflict and Cooperation: The Robbers Cave Experiment.* Norman, Okla.: University Book Exchange.

SILBERMAN, C. E. 1971. *Crisis in the Classroom.* New York: Vintage Books.

SINGER, D. 1967. The influence of intelligence and an interracial classroom on social attitudes. In R. A. Dentler, B. Mackler, and M. E. Warshauer, eds., *The Urban R's: Race Relations as the Problem in Urban Education.* New York: Praeger.

SLAVIN, R. 1974. The effects of teams in Teams-Games-Tournament on the normative climates of classrooms. Center for Social Organization of Schools, Johns Hopkins University.

SMITH, A. J., MADDEN, H. E., and SOBEL, R. 1957. Productivity and recall in cooperative and competitive discussion groups. *Journal of Psychology* 43:193–204.

SOROKIN, P. A., M. TRANQUIST, M. PARTEN, and C. C. ZIMMERMAN. 1930. An experimental study of efficiency of work under various specified conditions. *American Journal of Sociology* 35:765–82.

SPILERMAN, S. 1971. Raising academic motivation in lower class adolescents: a convergence of two research traditions. *Sociology of Education* 44:103–18.

STAUB, E. 1971. Helping a person in distress: the influence of implicit and explicit "rules" of conduct on children and adults. *Journal of Personality and Social Psychology* 17:137–44.

STENDLER, C., DAMRIN, D., and HAINES, A. 1951. Studies in cooperation and competition: I. the effects of working for group and individual rewards on the social climate of children's groups. *Journal of Genetic Psychology* 79:173–79.

SWINGLE, P. G., and H. COADY. 1967. Effects of the partner's abrupt strategy change upon subject's responding in the prisoner's dilemma. *Journal of Personality and Social Psychology* 5:357–63.

THELEN, H. A. 1970. A proposal for the attainment of racial integration through public education. *School Review* 391–96.

THOMAS, E. J. 1957. Effects of facilitative role interdependence on group functioning. *Human Relations* 10:347–66.

TRIPLETT, N. 1897. The dynamogenic factors in pacemaking and competition. *American Journal of Psychology* 9:507–33.

TSENG, S. C. 1969. An experimental study of the effect of three types of distribution of reward upon work efficiency and group dynamics. Unpublished doctoral dissertation, Columbia University.

UEJIO, C. K., and L. S. WRIGHTSMAN. 1967. Ethnic-group differences in the relationship of trusting attitudes to cooperative behavior. *Psychological Reports* 20:563–71.

WALBERG, H. J., and S. C. THOMAS. 1971. *Characteristics of open education: toward an operational definition.* Newton, Mass.: TDR Associates.

WATSON, G., and D. W. JOHNSON. 1972. *Social Psychology: Issues and Insights,* Second Edition. Philadelphia: J. B. Lippincott Co.

213

WEIGEL, R. H., P. L. WISER, and S. W. COOK. 1974. The impact of cooperative learning experiences on cross-ethnic relations and attitudes. Mimeographed report, University of Colorado, Institute of Behavioral Sciences.

WENT, F. W. 1963. *The Plants*. New York: Time, Inc.

WHEELER, R. C. 1972. A comparison of the effects of cooperative and competitive grouping situations on the perceptions, attitudes, and achievement of elementary school students engaged in social studies inquiry activities. Unpublished doctoral dissertation, University of Minnesota.

———, and F. L. RYAN. Effects of cooperative and competitive classroom environments on the attitudes and achievement of elementary school students engaged in social studies inquiry activities. *Journal of Educational Psychology*, 65:402–407.

WILHELMS, F. T. 1970. Educational conditions essential to growth in individuality. In V. M. Howes, ed., *Individualization of Instruction: A Teaching Strategy*. New York: The Macmillan Co.

WILLIS, R. H., and M. L. JOSEPH. 1959. Bargaining behavior. I: "prominence" as a predictor of the outcome of games of agreement. *Conflict Resolution* 3:102–13.

WILSON, W., and N. MILLER. 1961. Shifts in evaluation of participants following intergroup competition. *Journal of Abnormal and Social Psychology*, 63:428–432.

WITTE, P. H. 1972. The effects of group reward structure on interracial acceptance, peer tutoring, and academic performance. Unpublished doctoral dissertation, Washington University.

WODARSKI, J. S., R. L. HAMBLIN, D. BUCKHOLDT, and D. E. FERRITOR. 1971. Effects of individual and group contingencies on arithmetic performance. Paper presented at the meetings of the AERA, New York, 1971.

———. 1972. The effects of low performance group and individual contingencies on cooperative behaviors exhibited by fifth graders. *The Psychological Record* 22:359–68.

———. 1973. Individual consequences versus different shared consequences contingent on the performance of low-achieving group members. *Journal of Applied Social Psychology* 3:276–90.

———. 1974. Use of group reinforcement in school social work practice. *The Journal of School Social Work* 1:26–38.

YUKER, H. E. 1955. Group atmosphere and memory. *Journal of Abnormal and Social Psychology* 51:17–23.

ZAJONC, R. B., and I. C. MARIN. 1967. Cooperation, competition, and interpersonal attitudes in small groups. *Psychonomic Science* 7:271–72.